<u>QUOTES ON QUOTES</u>

The obvious is that which is never seen until someone expresses it simply. (K Gibran)

If I have seen further it is by standing on the shoulders of giants. (Sir Isaac Newton)

It is a good thing for an educated man to read books of quotations. (Sir Winston Churchill)

It is a pleasure to be able to quote lines to fit any occasion. (Abraham Lincoln)

ABILITY		Everybody is a genius. But if you judge a fish by its ability to climb a tree, it will live its whole life believing that it is stupid. (Albert Einstein)

ABILITY		The Creator has not given you a longing to do that which you have no ability to do. (OS Marden)

ABILITY		Ability will never catch up with the demand for it.		(Confucius)

ABILITY		There is something that is much more scarce, something rarer than ability. It is the ability to recognize ability. (Robert Half)

ABUNDANCE		Consider not the present condition, but rather foresee the future and the end. A seed in the beginning is very small, but in the end a great tree. One should not consider the seed, but the tree and its abundance of blossoms, leaves and fruits. (Abdul Baha)

ACCEPTANCE		Acceptance of one's life has nothing to do with resignation, it does not mean running away from the struggle. On the contrary, it means accepting it as it comes, with all the handicaps of heredity, of suffering of psychological complexes and injustices. (Paul Tournier)

ACCEPTANCE		First, see clearly. Next, act correctly. Finally, endure and accept the world as it is. (Ryan Holiday)

ACHIEVEMENT	In a wide variety of human activity, achievement is not possible without discomfort. (Alex Hutchinson)

ACHIEVEMENT	My mother drew a distinction between achievement and success. She said, "Achievement is the knowledge that you have studied and worked hard and done the best that is in you. Success is being praised by others. That is nice, too, but not as important or satisfying. Always aim for achievement and forget about success. (Helen Hayes)

ACTING ☺ Acting is all about honesty. If you can fake that, you have got it made. (Don Marquis)

ACTING ☺ I was lousy in school. Real screwed up. A moron. I was antisocial and didn't bother with the other kids. A really bad student. I didn't have any brains. I didn't know what I was doing there. That's why I became an actor. (Anthony Hopkins)

ACTING ☺ If someone was stupid enough to offer me a million dollars to make a picture, I am certainly not dumb enough to turn it down. (Elizabeth Taylor)

ACTING ☺ When they asked Jack Benny to do something for the Actor's Orphanage- he shot both his parents and moved in. (Bob Hope)

ACTION   Never confuse motion with action. (B Franklin)

ACTION   The most effective way to do it is to do it. (Amelia Earhart)

ACTION   The smallest deed is better than the greatest intention. (John Burroughs)

ACTION   You know what is better than building things up in your imagination? Building things up in real life. (Ryan Holiday)

ACTION   Even if you're on the right track, you'll get run over if you just sit there. (Will Rogers)

ACTION   I am only one, but still I am one. I cannot do everything but still I do something. I will not refuse to do the something I can do. (Helen Keller)

ACTION   I have been impressed with the urgency of doing. Knowing is not enough, we must apply. Being willing is not enough, we must do. (Leonardo Da Vinci)

ACTION   Inspirations never go in for long engagements, they demand immediate marriage to action. (B Francis)

ACTION   Never confuse motion with action. (Ernest Hemingway)

ACTION   The world is an oyster but you don't crack it open on a mattress. (Arthur Miller)

ACTION   The world is changed by your example not by your opinion. (Paulo Coelho)

ACTION   The world is more malleable than you think, and it's waiting for you to hammer it into shape. (Bono)

ACTION   When your work speaks for itself, don't interrupt. (Henry J. Kaiser)

ACTION   Words are plentiful, deeds are precious. (Lech Walsena)

ACTION   It takes less time to do a thing right than to explain why you did it wrong. (Longfellow)

ADVENTURE   If you think adventure is dangerous, try normal; its lethal. (Paulo Coelho)

ADVERSITY   We are all broken. That's how the light gets in. (Hemingway)

ADVERSITY ☺   If life gives you lemons, make lemonade...And try to find somebody whose life has given them vodka. (Ron White)

ADVERSITY   Adversity is the trial of principle. Without it a man hardly knows whether he is honest or not. (Henry Fielding)

ADVERSITY   The way I see it, if you want the rainbow, you gotta put up with the rain. (Dolly Parton)

ADVERTISING ☺   The only reason I made a commercial for American Express was to pay my American Express Bill. (Peter Ustinov)

ADVERTISING   Doing business without advertising is like winking at a girl in the dark. You know what you are doing but no one else does. (Stewart H Britt)

ADVERTISING   Few people at the beginning of the nineteenth century needed an adman to tell them what they wanted. (JK Galbraith)

ADVERTISING   It did what all ads are supposed to do: create an anxiety relievable by purchase. (David Foster Wallace)

ADVERTISING   The philosophy behind much advertising is based on the old observation that every man is really two men- the man he is and the man he wants to be. (William Feather)

ADVERTISING   We grew up founding our dreams on the infinite promise of American advertising. I still believe that one can learn to play the piano by mail and that mud will give you a perfect complexion. (Zelda Fitzgerald)

ADVERTISING   Advertising may be described as the science of arresting the human intelligence long enough to get money from it. (Stephen Leacock)

ADVICE   It is easy when we are in prosperity to give advice to the afflicted. (Aeschylus)

AFFAIR   I have been in love with the same woman for forty-one years. If my wife finds out, she will kill me. (Henry Youngman)

AFFECTION   Talk not of wasted affection. Affection never was wasted. (Henry W Longfellow)

AGE   You are never too old to set another goal or to dream a new dream. (CS Lewis)

AGE   I used to dread getting older because I thought I would not be able to do all the things I wanted to do, but now that I am older, I find that I don't want to do them. (Nancy Astor)

AGE   Probably the happiest period in life most frequently is in middle age, when the eager passions of youth are cooled, and the infirmities of age not yet begun, as we see that the shadows, which are at morning and evening so large, almost entirely disappear on midday. (Eleanor Roosevelt)

AGE   The fear of becoming old is born of the recognition that one is not living now the life that one wishes. It is equivalent to a sense of abusing the present. (Susan Sontag)

AGE   The oldest trees often bear the sweetest fruit. (German proverb)

AGE   When grace is joined with wrinkles ; it is adorable. There is an unspeakable dawn in happy old age. (Victor Hugo)

AGE ☺   I turned 24 last week. Pythagoras was 22 when he worked out the lengths of a right-angled triangle for the first time. I covered that in Year Six, so I am doing pretty bloody well. (Rob Oldham)

AGE   Age is not all decay ; it is the ripening, the swelling, of the fresh life within, that that withers and bursts the husk. (George Macdonald)

AGE   Age is something that does not matter, unless you are a cheese. (Luis Bunuel)

AGE   Anyone can get old. All you have to do is live long enough. (Groucho Marx)

AGE   Anyone who stops learning is old, whether at 20 or 80. Anyone who keeps learning stays young. (Henry Ford)

AGE   First you forget names then you forget faces, then you forget to pull your zipper up, then you forget to pull your zipper down. (Leo Rosenberg)

AGE   I am sixty-five and I guess that puts me in with the geriatrics, but if there were fifteen months in every year, I would only be forty-eight. (James Thurber)

AGE   I refuse to admit I am more than fifty-two even if that does make my sons illegitimate. (Lady Astor)

AGE   If I had known I was gonna live this long, I would have taken better care of myself. (E Blake)

AGE   It is paradoxical that the idea of living a long life appeals to everyone, but the idea of getting old does not appeal to anyone. (Andy Rooney)

AGE   It takes a very long time to become young. (Pablo Picasso)

AGE   Jewellery takes peoples' minds off your wrinkles. (Sonja Henie)

AGE ☺   Older people shouldn't eat health food, they need all the preservatives they can get. (Robert Orben)

AGE   The excitement of learning separates youth from old age. As long as you are learning you are not old. (Rosalyn S Yalow)

AGE   The secret of staying young is to live honestly, eat slowly, and lie about your age. (Lucille Ball)

AGE   The young man knows the rules, but the old man knows the exceptions. (Oliver Wendell Holmes, Sr.)

AGE   To grow old is to pass from passion to compassion. (A Camus)

AGE   To me, old age is fifteen years older than I am. (BM Baruch)

AGE   When your friends begin to flatter you on how young you look, it is a sure sign you are getting old. (Mark Twain)

AGE   You have heard of the three ages of man : youth, middle age, and 'you are looking wonderful'. (Francis Joseph)

AGE ☺   You know you are getting old when the candles cost more than the cake. (Bob Hope)

AGE   Young men want to be faithful and are not ; old men want to be faithless and cannot. (Oscar Wilde)

AGE   Youth cannot know how age thinks and feels. But old men are guilty if they forget what it was to be young. (JK Rowling)

AGONY   There is no greater agony than bearing an untold story inside you. (Maya Angelou)

AI   Nobody phrases it this way, but I think that artificial intelligence is almost a humanities discipline. It's really an attempt to understand human intelligence and human cognition. (Sebastian Thrun)

AI   A year spent in Artificial Intelligence is enough to make one believe in God. (Alan Perlis)

AI   Before we work on Artificial Intelligence, why don't we do something about natural stupidity? (Steve Polyak)

ALONE   Poverty only tries men's souls. It is loneliness that breaks the heart. (Sam Rayburn)

AMBITION   Ambition is a dream with a V8 engine. (Elvis)

AMBITION   It is never too late to be what you might have been. (George Eliot)

AMBITION A man's worth is no greater than his ambitions. (Marcus Aurelius)

AMBITION Ambition is best not naked. (M Forbes)

AMBITION Reach for the stars, even if you have to stand on a cactus. (Susan Longacre)

ANGEL   Angels can fly because they take themselves lightly, devils fall because of their gravity. (GK Chesterton)

ANGER   Anger is an acid that can do more harm to the vessel in which it is stored than to anything on which it is poured. (Mark Twain)

ANGER   For every minute you are angry, you lose sixty seconds of happiness. (RW Emerson)

ANGER   I never work better than when I am inspired by anger, for when I am angry, I can write, pray, and preach well, for then my whole temperament is quickened, my understanding sharpened, and all mundane vexations and temptations depart. (Martin Luther)

ANGER   Never forget what someone says to you when they are angry. (Henry Ward Beecher)

ANGER   Whining is anger through a small opening. (Al Franken)

ANXIETY   Anxiety is the dizziness of freedom. (Søren Kierkegaard)

APOLOGY Never ruin an apology with an excuse. (B Franklin)

APOLOGY Never apologize for showing feeling. When you do so, you apologize for truth. (Benjamin Disraeli)

APPEARANCE ☺   I never go outside unless I look like Joan Crawford the movie star. If you want to see the girl next door, go next door. (Joan Crawford)

APPEASEMENT   An appeaser is one who feeds a crocodile, hoping it will eat him last. (Winston Churchill)

APPRECIATION   Appreciation is a wonderful thing. It makes what is excellent in others belong to us as well. (Voltaire)

ARGUMENT   Discussion is an exchange of knowledge, argument an exchange of ignorance. (Robert Quillen)

ART   A work of art that contains theories is like an object on which the price tag has been left. (Alexander Pope)

ART   Art is the stored honey of the human soul, gathered on wings of misery and travail. (Theodore Dreiser)

ART   Don't think about making art, just get it done. Let everyone else decide if it's good or bad, whether they love it or hate it. While they are deciding, make even more art. (Andy Warhol)

ART   It is a mistake for a sculptor or a painter to speak or write very often about his job. It releases tension needed for his work. (Henry Moore)

ART   An art can only be learnt in the workshop of those who are winning their bread by it. (Samuel Butler)

ART   Art never responds to the wish to make it democratic; it is not for everybody; it is only for those who are willing to undergo the effort needed to understand it. (Flannery O'Connor)

ART   For me, painting is a way to forget life. It is a cry in the night, a strangled laugh. (G Rouault)

ART   In nature, light creates the colour. In the picture, colour creates the light. (Hans Hofmann)

ART   The world does not make sense, so why should I paint pictures that do. (Pablo Picasso)

ART   There are three forms of visual art : Painting is art to look at, sculpture is art you can walk around, and architecture is art you can walk through. (Dan Rice)

ART   To say that a work of art is good, but incomprehensible to the majority of men, is the same as saying of some kind of food that it is very good but that most people can't eat it. (Leo Tolstoy)

ART   To the accountants, a true work of art is an investment that hangs on the wall. (Hilary Alexander)

ARTIST   Artists are people driven by the tension between the desire to communicate and the desire to hide. (DW Winnicott)

ARTIST   He who works with his hands is a laborer. He who works with his hands and his head is a craftsman. He who works with his hands and his head and his heart is an artist. (St. Francis of Assisi)

ARTIST   If you ask me what I came to do in this world, I, an artist, will answer you: I am here to live out loud. (Émile Zola)

ARTIST   It is not always the best artists that garner the greatest sales, but the best marketers of their art. (Brian Knowles)

ARTIST   No one should drive a hard bargain with an artist. (Beethoven)

ASSUMPTION   Your assumptions are your windows on the world. Scrub them off every once in a while, or the light won't come in. (Isaac Asimov)

ASTRONAUT   When you are getting ready to launch into space, you are sitting on a big explosion just waiting to happen. (Sally Ride)

ATHEIST   The worst moment for the atheist is when he is really thankful and has nobody to thank. (Dante)

ATTENTION   The moment one gives close attention to anything, even a blade of grass, it becomes a mysterious, awesome, indescribably magnificent world in itself. (Henry Miller)

ATTIRE ☺ A woman's dress should be like a barbed-wire fence, serving its purpose without obstructing the view. (Sophia Loren)

ATTITUDE If you view things that happen to you, both good and bad, as opportunities, then you operate out of a higher level of consciousness. (Les Brown)

ATTITUDE If you cry because the sun has gone out of your life, your tears will prevent you from seeing the stars. (R Tagore)

ATTITUDE The greatest discovery of my generation is that human beings can alter their lives by altering their attitudes of mind. (W James)

ATTITUDE Ability is what you're capable of doing. Motivation determines what you do. Attitude determines how well you do it. (Raymond Chandler)

ATTITUDE If you want to change attitudes, start with a change in behaviours. (Katharine Hepburn)

ATTITUDE People may hear your words, but they feel your attitude. (John C Maxwell)

AUDIENCE The best audience is one that is intelligent, well-educated- and a little drunk. (AW Barkley)

AUTOCRAT No one can go on being a rebel too long without turning into an autocrat. (Laurence Durrell)

AWARD Awards are like haemorrhoids, once in a lifetime every asshole gets one. (Billy Wilder)

AWARD Getting an award from TV is like getting kissed by someone with bad breath. (Mason Williams)

AWARENESS Every time you spend money, you are casting a vote for the kind of world you want. (Anna Lappe)

BABY The toddler craves independence, but he fears desertion. (DC Briggs)

BABY People who say they sleep like a baby usually don't have one. (Leo J. Burke)

BANK   A bank is a place where they lend you an umbrella in fair weather and ask for it back when it begins to rain. (Robert Frost)

BANKRUPTCY ☺   It is said that the world is in a state of bankruptcy, that the world owes the world more than the world can pay. (RW Emerson)

BEAUTY   Nothing makes a woman more beautiful than the belief that she is beautiful. (Sophia Loren)

BEAUTY   The beauty of a living thing is not the atoms that go into it, but the way those atoms are put together. (Carl Sagan)

BEAUTY ☺ Beauty is in the eye of the beholder and it may be necessary from time to time to give a stupid or misinformed beholder a black eye. (Jim Henson)

BEAUTY ☺ Everything you see I owe to pasta. (Sophia Loren)

BEAUTY   For beautiful eyes, look for the good in others ; for beautiful lips, speak only words of kindness ; and for poise, walk with the knowledge that you are never alone. (Audrey Hepburn)

BEAUTY   I never saw an ugly thing in my life : for let the form of an object be what it may, -light, shade, and perspective will always make it beautiful. (John Constable)

BEAUTY   It is amazing how complete is the delusion that beauty is goodness. (Leo Tolstoy)

BEAUTY   The beauty of a woman is seen in her eyes, because that is the doorway to her heart, the place where love resides. (Audrey Hepburn)

BEGINNING   The creation of a thousand forests is in one acorn. (RW Emerson)

BEGINNING   The man who goes alone can start today; but he who travels with another must wait till that other is ready. (Henry David Thoreau)

BEHAVIOUR   An abnormal reaction to an abnormal situation is normal behavior. (Viktor Frankl)

BLESSING Make blessing others part of your work day. (Mary Davis)

BLISS   It is good to be just plain happy, it is a little better to know that you are happy, but to understand that you are happy and to know why and how and still be happy, be happy in the being and the knowing, well that is beyond happiness, that is bliss. (Henry Miller)

BOLDNESS   Whatever you do, or dream you can, begin it. Boldness has genius and power and magic in it. (Goethe)

BOOK   Successful people have libraries. The rest have big screen TVs. (Jim Rohn)

BOOK   I cannot remember the books I've read any more than the meals I have eaten; even so, they have made me. (Ralph Waldo Emerson)

BOOK   A book is a dream that you hold in your hand. (Neil Gaiman)

BOOK   There is no friend as loyal as a book. (Ernest Hemingway)

BOOKS   Books are the carriers of civilization. Without books, history is silent, literature dumb, science crippled, thought and speculation at a standstill. Without books, the development of civilization would have been impossible. They are engines of change (as the poet said), windows on the world and lighthouses erected in the sea of time. They are companions, teachers, magicians, bankers of the treasures of the mind. Books are humanity in print. (Barbara Tuchman)

BOOKS   Books serve to show a man that those original thoughts of his aren't very new after all. (Abraham Lincoln)

BOOKS   He never went out without a book under his arm, and he often came back with two. (Victor Hugo)

BOOKS   Never lend books, for no one ever returns them, the only books I have in my library are books that other folks have lent me. (Anatole France)

BOOKS   Read the best books first, or you may not have a chance to read them at all. (HD Thoreau)

BOOKS   Readers are of two sorts, one who carefully goes through a book, and the other who as carefully lets the book go through him. (Douglas Jerrold)

BOOKS   The library is an arena of possibility opening both a window into the soul and a door onto the world. (Rita Dove)

BOOKS   The reading of all good books is like a conversation with the finest men of past centuries. (Rene Descartes)

BOOKS   When you read a classic, you do not see more in the book than you did before, you see more in you than there was before. (Clifton Fadiman)

BOOKS   Books are the bees which carry the quickening pollen from one to another mind. (JR Lowell)

BORE   A bore is a man who, when you ask him how he is, tells you. (BL Taylor)

BORE   Everyone is a bore to someone. That is unimportant. The thing to avoid is being a bore to oneself. (Gerald Brenan)

BRAG   The man who must brag for himself knows that no one else will. (Robin Hobb)

BREVITY   It is my ambition to say in ten sentences what others say in a whole book. (Friedrich Nietzsche)

BUDGET   Don't tell me what you value, show me your budget, and I will tell you what you value. (Joe Biden)

BUDGET   Just as we should never balance the budget on the backs of the poor, so it is an economic delusion to think you can balance it only on the wallets of the rich. (George Osborne)

BUDGET   Normally, when politicians talk about 'cutting the budget', they really mean reducing the amount of increase. Actual spending goes up while the politicians claim to have 'cut the budget'. (Mark McKinnon)

BUDGET   The budget does not have much control over the government. Then again, the government does not have much control over the budget. (PJ O'Rourke)

BUDGET   The budget evolved from a management tool into an obstacle to management. (Frank Carlucci)

BUREAUCRACY   Bureaucracy is a giant mechanism operated by pygmies. (H Balzac)

BUREAUCRACY ☺ Red tape will often get in your way. It is one of the reasons I often carry scissors. (Richard Branson)

BUSINESS A business that makes nothing but money is a poor business. (Henry Ford)

BUSINESS A businessman is a hybrid of a dancer and a calculator. (Paul Valery)

BUSINESS Fuel is not sold in a forest, nor fish on a lake. (Chinese proverb)

BUSINESS Hire people who are better than you are, then leave them to get on with it. (David Ogilvy)

BUSINESS His quest for something new each month leads to widespread corporate premature ejaculation. (Robert Townsend)

BUSINESS If you bet on a horse, that is gambling. If you bet you can make three spades, that is entertainment. If you bet cotton will go up three points, that is business. See the difference? (Blackie Sherrode)

BUSINESS In business, when two people always agree, one of them is irrelevant. (William Wrigley)

BUSINESS In the end, all business operations can be reduced to three words : people, product and profits. Unless you have got a good team, you can't do much with the other two. (Lee Iacocca)

BUSINESS It is not from the benevolence of the butcher, the brewer, or the baker that we expect our dinner, but from their regard to their own interest. (Adam Smith)

BUSINESS Scratch the surface in a typical boardroom and we are all just cavemen with briefcases, hungry for a wise person to tell our stories. (Alan Kay)

BUSINESS The business end of business has never interested me. (Hugh Hefner)

BUSINESS What gets measured gets improved. (Peter Drucker)

CAPITAL The highest use of capital is not to make more money, but to make money to do more for the betterment of life. (Henry Ford)

CAPITALISM The only thing worse than being exploited by capitalism is not being exploited by capitalism. (JV Robinson)

CAPITALISM The oppressed are allowed once every few years to decide which particular representatives of the oppressing class are to represent and repress them. (Karl Marx)

CARE To make a difference in someone's life, you don't have to be brilliant, rich, beautiful or perfect. You just have to care. (Mandy Hale)

CARE When you remember something about somebody, you are demonstrating to them that you care. (Joshua Foer)

CARE You know how they say we only use 10 percent of our brains? I think we only use 10 percent of our hearts. (Owen Wilson)

CAREFREE I want to sing like the birds sing, not worrying about who hears or what they think. (Rumi)

CAREFREE You think that through a self-imposed asceticism you will increase your awareness and then be able to use that awareness to be happy. No chance. You will be peaceful when all your ideas about awareness are dropped and you begin to function like a computer. (UG Krishnamurti)

CAT   Cats are intended to teach us that not everything in nature has a function. (G Keillor)

CAT   If a dog jumps in your lap, it is because he is fond of you; but if a cat does the same thing, it is because your lap is warmer. (AN Whitehead)

CAT ☺   Anyone who considers protocol unimportant has never dealt with a cat. (RA Heinlein)

CELEBRITY   A celebrity is a person who works hard all his life to become well known, and then wears dark glasses to avoid being recognized. (Fred Allen)

CELEBRITY   In rock stardom, there is an absolute economic upside to self-destruction. (Courtney Love)

CENSORSHIP   To limit the press is to insult a nation, to prohibit reading of certain books is to declare the inhabitants to be either fools or slaves. (CA Helvetius)

CERTAINTY   I am certain there is too much certainty in the world. (Michael Crichton)

CHALLENGE   We cannot change the cards we are dealt, just how we play the hand. (Randy Pausch)

CHALLENGE ☺   When life gives you lemons, squirt someone in the eye. (Cathy Guisewite)

CHALLENGE   Upheavals sieve the big men from the little. (BC Forbes)

CHALLENGE   When the wind rises some people build walls. Others build windmills. (Chinese proverb)

CHALLENGE   Kites rise highest against the wind, not with it. (Winston S. Churchill)

CHALLENGE   The only real limitation is the one you accept & set up in your own mind. (Napoleon Hill)

CHALLENGE   You pray for the rain, you gotta deal with the mud too. That's a part of it. (Denzel Washington)

CHAMPION   A champion is someone who gets up when he can't. (Jack Dempsey)

CHANGE   Change is the law of life. And those who look only to the past or present are certain to miss the future. (John F Kennedy)

CHANGE   The secret of change is to focus all of your energy, not on fighting the old, but on building the new. (Dan Millman)

CHANGE   Truth always originates in a minority of one, and every custom begins as a broken precedent. (Nancy Astor)

CHANGE   We delight in the beauty of the butterfly, but rarely admit the changes it has gone through to achieve that beauty. (Maya Angelou)

CHANGE   We generally change ourselves for one of two reasons: inspiration or desperation. (Jim Rohn)

CHANGE   Faced with the choice between changing one's mind and proving that there is no need to do so, almost everyone gets busy on the proof. (JK Galbraith)

CHANGE   The secret to change is to focus all of your energy, not on fighting the old, but on building the new. (Socrates)

CHANGE   There is no way to make people like change. You can only make them feel less threatened by it. (FO Hayes)

CHANGE   Usually when people are sad, they don't do anything. They just cry over their condition. But when they get angry, they bring about a change. (Malcolm X)

CHANGE   We delight in the beauty of the butterfly, but rarely admit the changes it has gone through to achieve that beauty. (Maya Angelou)

CHANGE   Change is hard at first, messy in the middle and gorgeous at the end. (Robin Sharma)

CHANGE   In the midst of change we often discover wings we never knew we had. (Ekaterina Walter)

CHANGE   The art of progress is to preserve order amid change and to preserve change amid order. (AN Whitehead)

CHANGE   The displacement of a little sand can change occasionally the course of a deep river. (MG Prada)

CHARACTER   A man never discloses his own character so clearly as when he describes another's. (JP Richter)

CHARACTER   Character cannot be developed in ease and quiet. Only through experience of trial and suffering can the soul be strengthened, ambition inspired, and success achieved. (Helen Keller)

CHARACTER   Character is like pregnancy. It cannot be hidden forever. (African proverb)

CHARACTER   Character is what God and the angels know of us, reputation is what men and women think of us. (Horace Mann)

CHARACTER   Character may almost be called the most effective means of persuasion. (Aristotle)

CHARACTER   Character may be manifested in the great moments, but it is made in the small ones. (Winston Churchill)

CHARACTER   No one has ever made himself great by showing how small someone else is. (Irvin Himmel)

CHARACTER   People do not seem to realise that their opinion of the world is also a confession of character. (RW Emerson)

CHARACTER   You cannot dream yourself into a character, you must hammer and forge yourself into one. (Henry D. Thoreau)

CHARACTER   Character is much easier kept than recovered. (Thomas Paine)

CHARACTER   In each human heart are a tiger a pig, an ass and a nightingale. DIversity of character is due to their unequal activity. (A Bierce)

CHARITY Better do a good deed near at home than go far away to burn incense. (Amelia Earhart)

CHARITY Charity is injurious unless it helps the recipient to become independent of it. (JD Rockefeller)

CHARITY True charity is the desire to be useful to others with no thought of recompense. (Emanuel Swedenborg)

CHARITY   No one would remember the Good Samaritan if he only had good intentions. He had money as well. (Margaret Thatcher)

CHEERFUL   You find yourself refreshed by the presence of cheerful people. Why not make an honest effort to confer that pleasure on others? Half the battle is gained if you never allow yourself to say anything gloomy. (Julia Child)

CHILD   A child's eyes, those clear wells of undefiled thought..what on earth can be more beautiful? Full of hope, love and curiosity, they meet your own. (Caroline Norton)

CHILD   Any kid will run any errand for you, if you ask at bedtime. (Red Skelton)

CHILD   Children have never been very good at listening to their elders, but they have never failed to imitate. (James Baldwin)

CHILD   Children's talent to endure stems from their ignorance of alternatives. (Maya Angelou)

CHILD   Every child deserves a champion- an adult who will never give up on them, who understands the power of connection and insists that they become the best that they can possibly be. (Rita Pierson)

CHILD   The most important things a child can inherit are fond memories. (F Sonnenberg)

CHILD   A three-year-old child is a being who gets almost as much fun out of a fifty-six dollar set of swings as it does out of finding a small green worm. (Bill Vaughan)

CHILD   Because of their size, parents may be difficult to discipline properly. (Pablo Picasso)

CHILD   Children are great comfort in your old age and they help you reach it faster too. (Lionel Kauffman)

CHILD   In every child who is born, under no matter what circumstances, and of no matter what parents, the potentiality of the human race is born again. (James Agee)

CHILD   Insanity is hereditary, you can get it from your children. (Sam Levenson)

CHILD   It is easier to build strong children than to repair broken men. (Frederick Douglass)

CHILD   There are only two lasting bequests we can hope to give our children. One of these is roots, the other, wings. (Hodding carter)

CHILDHOOD   I believe that what we become depends on what our fathers teach us at odd moments, when they aren't trying to teach us. We are formed by little scraps of wisdom. (Umberto Eco)

CHILDREN Children are made readers on the laps of their parents. (Emilie Bunchwald)

CHILDREN Each new generation born is in effect an invasion of civilization by little barbarians, who must be civilized before it is too late. (Thomas Sowell)

CHILDREN While we try to teach our children all about life, our children teach us what life is all about. (Angela Schwindt)

CHOICE   All courses of action are risky, so prudence is not in avoiding danger (it's impossible), but calculating risk and acting decisively. Make mistakes of ambition and not mistakes of sloth. Develop the strength to do bold things, not the strength to suffer. (Niccolò Machiavelli)

CHOICE   Which form of proverb do you prefer, better late than never, or better never than late? (Lewis Carroll)

CHOICE   It is our choices that show what we truly are, far more than our abilities. (J.K. Rowling)

CHOICE   There is no such thing as work-life balance. There are work-life choices, and you make them, and they have consequences. (Jack Wlech)

CIRCUMSTANCES The winds and waves are always on the side of the ablest navigators. (Edward Gibbon)

CITIZEN   Never doubt that a small group of thoughtful, committed citizens can change the world ; indeed, it is the only thing that ever has. (Margaret Mead)

CIVILITY   We are born princes and the civilizing process turns us into frogs. (Eric Berne)

CLIMATE   Twenty-five years ago, people could be excused for not knowing much, or doing much, about climate change. Today we have no excuse. (Desmond Tutu)

COINCIDENCE   Coincidence is God's way of remaining anonymous. (Albert Einstein)

COMEDY   It is easy being a humorist when you have got the whole government working for you. (Will Rogers)

COMMITMENT   The best way to keep your word is not to give it. (Napoleon Bonaparte)

COMMUNICATION   Dialogue cannot exist without humility. (Paulo Freire)

COMMUNICATION   What is uttered from the heart alone will win the hearts of others to your own. (Goethe)

COMMUNICATION   Communication is something so simple and difficult that we can never put it in simple words. (TS Matthews)

COMMUNICATION   Good communication is as stimulating as black coffee, and just as hard to sleep after. (Anne M Lindbergh)

COMMUNICATION   Human communication permeates the human condition. Human communication surrounds us and is an in-built aspect of everything human beings are and do. That makes any effort to explain, predict, to some extent control human communication a pretty big order. How does one get a handle on the totality of human communication? (Frank Dance)

COMMUNICATION   I sometimes feel I have nothing to say, and I want to communicate this. (Damien Hirst)

COMMUNICATION   Science may never come up with a better office communication system than the coffee break. (Earl Wilson)

COMMUNICATION   The Art of communication is the language of leadership. (James Humes)

COMPANY Friends and good manners will carry you where money won't go. (Margaret Walker)

COMPASSION   If your compassion does not include yourself, it is incomplete. (Buddha)

COMPETITION   Never compete with someone who has nothing to lose. (B Gracian)

COMPETITION   A horse never runs so fast as when he has other horses to catch up and outpace. (Ovid)

COMPETITION   Competition brings out the best in products and the worst in people. (David Sarnoff)

COMPETITION   Competition is a rude yet effective motivation. (Toba Beta)

COMPETITION   If you are not gonna go all the way, why go at all? (Joe Namath)

COMPETITION   Rivalry is the life of trade, and death of the trader. (E Hubbard)

COMPETITION   The time your game is most vulnerable is when you are ahead. Never let up. (Rod Laver)

COMPOSURE   The way to find a needle in a haystack is to sit down. (Beryl Markham)

COMPROMISE   Compromise makes a good umbrella but a poor roof ; it is a temporary expedient. (JR Lowell)

COMPUTER   A computer would deserve to be called intelligent if it could deceive a human into believing that it was human. (Alan Turing)

COMPUTER   People think computers will keep them from making mistakes. They are wrong. With computers, you make mistakes faster. (Adam Osborne)

COMUNICATION The medium is the message. (Marshall McLuhan)

CONCEPT Every word or concept, clear as it may seem to be, has only a limited range of applicability. (Werner Heisenberg)

CONFIDENCE   Trust yourself. You know more than you think you do. (Benjamin Spock)

CONFIDENCE   When you have confidence, you can have a lot of fun. And when you have fun, you can do amazing things. (Joe Namath)

CONFIDENCE   If you think you can do a thing or think you can't do a thing, you are right. (Henry Ford)

CONFIDENCE   Stop acting so small. You are the universe in ecstatic motion. (Rumi)

CONFUSION ☺   If confusion is the first step to knowledge, I must be a genius. (Larry Leissner)

CONNECTION ☺   If you want to make an apple pie from scratch, you must first create the universe. (Carl Sagan)

CONSCIENCE   Conscience was born when man had shed his fur, his tail, his pointed ears. (Sir Richard Burton)

CONSCIOUSNESS The overall level of an ocean is not altered by the height of the waves at its surface. Our essential consciousness, similarly, remains unaffected y our emotional ups and downs. Pleasure-pain, and success-failure, are but waves on the surface of calm, intuitive feeling. (Swami Kriyananda)

CONSCIOUSNESS The real is ever-present. While the picture appears on it, the screen remains invisible. Stop the picture and the screen will become clear. All thoughts and events are merely pictures moving on the screen of Pure Consciousness, which alone is real. (Ramana Maharshi)

CONSUMERISM   What sets wilderness apart in the modern day is not that it's dangerous (it's almost certainly safer than any town or road) or that it's solitary (you can, so they say, be alone in a crowded room) or full of exotic animals (there are more at the zoo). It's that five miles out in the woods you can't buy anything. (Bill McKibben)

CONTENTMENT   Dissatisfaction is like a cancer of the spirit. It eats away at every possibility of love and joy. (Marty Rubin)

CONTENTMENT   Learn to be happy with what you have while your pursue all that you want. (Jim Rohn)

CONTRACT   It is a very sobering feeling to be up in space and realize that one's safety factor was determined by the lowest bidder on a government contract. (Alan Shepherd)

CONVERSATION   There is no conversation more boring than the one where everybody agrees. (Montaigne)

COOKING Non-cooks think it is silly to invest two hours' work in two minutes' enjoyment; but if cooking is evanescent, so is the ballet. (Julia Child)

CORPORATION   Corporations have neither bodies to be kicked nor souls to be damned. (Andrew Jackson)

CORPORATION   Corporations, which should be the carefully restrained creatures of the law and the servants of the people, are fast becoming the people's masters. (Grover Cleveland)

COURAGE Courage is tiny pieces of fear all glued together. (Terri Guillemets)

COURAGE It is curious that physical courage should be so common in the world and moral courage so rare. (Mark Twain)

COURAGE The most difficult thing is the decision to act, the rest is merely tenacity. The fears are paper tigers. You can do anything you decide to do. You can act to change and control your life, and the procedure, the process is its own reward. (Amelia Earhart)

COURAGE The only tyrant I accept in this world is the 'still small voice' within me. And even though I have to face the prospect of being a minority of one, I humbly believe I have the courage to be in such a hopeless minority. (Mahatma Gandhi)

COURAGE To dare is to lose one's footing momentarily. Not to dare is to lose oneself. (Soren Kierkegaard)

COURAGE True courage is not the brutal force of vulgar heroes, but the firm resolve of virtue and reason. (AN Whitehead)

COURAGE Courage stands halfway between cowardice and rashness, one of which is a lack, the other an excess of courage. (Plutarch)

COURAGE It is a blessed thing that in every age someone has had the individuality enough and courage enough to stand by his own convictions. (Robert G. Ingersoll)

COURAGE It is curious that physical courage should be so common in the world and moral courage so rare. (Mark Twain)

COURAGE The most courageous act is still to think for yourself. Aloud. (Coco Chanel)

COURAGE The opposite of courage in our society isn't cowardice, it's conformity. (Rollo May)

COURAGE To dare is to lose one's footing momentarily. Not to dare is to lose oneself. (Søren Kierkegaard)

COURT ☺ In almost every case, you have to read between the lies. (Angie Papadakis)

COURTESY Life is short, but there is always time enough for courtesy. (RW Emerson)

COWARD Cowardice, as distinguished from panic, is almost always simply a lack of ability to suspend the functioning of the imagination. (E Hemingway)

CREATION The whole difference between construction and creation is exactly this, that a thing constructed can only be loved after it is constructed, but a thing created is loved before it exists. (GK Chesterton)

CREATIVITY Anxiety is the handmaiden of creativity. (TS Eliot)

CREATIVITY Creativity is just connecting things. When you ask creative people how they did something, they feel a little guilty because they did not really do it, they just saw something. It seemed obvious to them after a while. (Steve Jobs)

CREATIVITY There is the happiness which comes from creative effort. The joy of dreaming, creating, building, whether in painting a picture, writing an epic, singing a song, composing a symphony, devising new invention, creating a vast industry. (Henry Miller)

CREATIVITY When Alexander the Great visited Diogenes and asked whether he could do anything for the famed teacher, Diogenes replied, 'Only stand out of my light.' Perhaps someday we shall know how to heighten creativity. Until then, one of the best things we can do for creative men and women is to stand out of their light. (JW Gardner)

CREATIVITY Activity itself is neither creative nor uncreative. You can paint in an uncreative way. You can sing in an uncreative way. You can clean the floor or cook in a creative way. Creativity is the quality that you bring to the activity you are doing. (Osho)

CREATIVITY   Creativity is so delicate a flower that praise tends to make it bloom, while discouragement often nips it in the bud. Any of us will put out more and better ideas if our efforts are appreciated. (AF Osborn)

CREDIT   When I was young, people lived from pay-cheque to pay-cheque. Today, it seems like they live from credit card payment to credit card payment. (Robert Kiyosaki)

CRIME   It makes a great difference whether a person is unwilling to sin, or does not know how. (Seneca)

CRITIC ☺   I, along with the critics, have never taken myself very seriously. (Elizabeth Taylor)

CRITIC   Young people need models, not critics. (John Wooden)

CRITICISM   Criticism is dangerous, because it wounds a person's precious pride, hurt his sense of importance and arouses resentment. (Dale Carnegie)

CRITICISM ☺   Before you criticize someone, you should walk a mile in their shoes. That way, when you criticize them, you are a mile away from them and have their shoes. (Jack Handey)

CRITICISM Criticism may not be agreeable, but it is necessary. It fulfils the same function as pain in the human body. It calls attention to an unhealthy state of things. (Winston Churchill)

CRITICISM Never attack the Performer, attack his Performance. (Lou Holtz)

CRITICISM There is only one way to avoid criticism : do nothing, say nothing , and be nothing. (Aristotle)

CRUELTY   Some things are not forgivable. Deliberate cruelty is not forgivable. It is the most unforgiveable thing in my opinion, and the one thing in which I have never, ever been guilty. (Tennessee Williams)

CRUELTY   Cruelty must be whitewashed by a moral excuse, and pretence of reluctance. (GB Shaw)

CRYING   If you have not cried, your eyes cannot be beautiful. (Sophia Loren)

CRYING   If you've never eaten while crying you don't know what life tastes like. (Goethe)

CRYPTOCURRENCY   Everything you don't understand about money combined with everything you don't understand about computers. (John Oliver)

CURIOSITY   It is a miracle that curiosity survives formal education. (Albert Einstein)

CURIOSITY   A sense of curiosity is nature's original school of education. (Smiley Blanton)

CURIOSITY   I have no special talent. I am only passionately curious. (Albert Einstein)

CYNIC   Cynicism is an unpleasant way of saying the truth. (Lillian Hellman)

DANCE   Dance is the hidden language of the soul. (Martha Graham)

DANCE   The job of feet is walking, but their hobby is dancing. (Amit Kalantri)

DATA   It's a basic, intuitive right, worthy of enshrinement: Citizens, not the corporations that stealthily track them, should own their own data. (Franklin Foer)

DATING ☺ Thanks to autocorrect, I sent my personal trainer a text asking if he fancied going for a rub on Sunday – obviously what I meant to say was Saturday. (Cally Beaton)

DEATH   Death does not concern us, because as long as we exist, death is not here. And when it does come, we no longer exist. (Epicurus)

DEATH   Death must be so beautiful. To lie in the soft brown earth with the grasses waving above one's head, and listen to silence. To have no yesterday, and no tomorrow. To forget time, to forgive life, to be at peace. (Oscar Wilde)

DEATH   Many people die at twenty-five and are not buried until they are seventy-five. (B Franklin)

DEATH   Our death is not an end if we can live on in our children and the younger generation. For they are us, our bodies are only wilted leaves on the tree of life. (Albert Einstein)

DEATH   The bitterest tears shed over graves are for words left unsaid and deeds left undone. (HB Stowe)

DEATH   Death gives meaning to our lives. It gives importance to time. Time is meaningless if there were too much of it. (Ray Kurzwell)

DEATH   Death is not the greatest loss in life. The greatest loss is what dies inside us while we live. ((Norman Cousins)

DEATH   I am not afraid to die. I just don't want to be there when it happens. (Woody Allen)

DEATH   It is hard to turn the page when you know someone won't be in the next chapter, but the story must go on. (Thomas Wilder)

DECEIT   They muddy the water, to make it seem deep. (Nietzsche)

DECISION It is hard to imagine a more stupid or more dangerous way of making decisions than by putting those decisions in the hands of people who pay no price for being wrong. (Thomas Sewell)

DECISION Nothing is more difficult, and therefore more precious, than to be able to decide. (Napoleon Bonaparte)

DECISION ☺   It is nice to make heroic decisions and to be prevented by 'circumstances beyond your control' from ever trying to execute them. (W James)

DECISION Even a correct decision is wrong when it is taken too late. (Lee Iacocca)

DECISION People will do things in a boardroom that they would never do as an individual. Group decisions, no personal liability. (Richard Schaden)

DEFEAT   Somewhere in the world there is a defeat for everyone. Some are destroyed by defeat, and some made small and mean by victory. Greatness lives in one who triumphs equally over defeat and victory. (John Steinbeck)

DEFEAT   We may encounter many defeats but we must not be defeated. (Maya Angelou)

DELEGATION   I have an absolute rule. I refuse to make a decision that somebody else can make. The first rule of leadership is to save yourself for the big decision. Don't allow your mind to become cluttered with the trivia. Don't let yourself become the issue. (Richard Nixon)

DEMOCRACY   A democracy is nothing more than mob rule, where fifty-one percent of the people may take away the rights of the other forty-nine. (Thomas Jefferson)

DEMOCRACY   Democracy   consists   of choosing your dictators, after they have told you what you think it is you want to hear. (Alan Coren)

DEMOCRACY   Democracy is a kingless regime infested by many kings who are sometimes more exclusive, tyrannical, and destructive than one, if he be a tyrant. (Benito Mussolini)

DEMOCRACY   Democracy is two wolves and a lamb voting on what to have for lunch. Liberty is a well-armed lamb contesting the vote. (Benjamin Franklin)

DENIAL   When a person tells you,"I will think it over and let you know" – you know. (Olin Miller)

DESIGN   Content precedes design. Design in the absence of content is not design, it's decoration. (Jeffrey Zeldman)

DESIGN   Design is not crafting a beautiful, textured button with breathtaking animation. It is figuring out if there is a way to get rid of the button altogether. (E Tufte)

DESIRE   Desire makes everything blossom, possession makes everything wither and fade. (M Proust)

DESIRE   A person can attain peace only if he is not affected by continuous flow of desires. If he tries to satisfy such desires, he will not be at peace. Desires are like rivers and mind is like an ocean. Just like ocean remains still after rivers enter the ocean, mind needs to remain still when desires enter. (The Gita 2/70)

DETERMINATION Set your mind on a definite goal and observe how quickly the world stands aside to let you pass. (Napoleon Hill)

DIAMOND A diamond is merely a lump of coal that did well under pressure. (Henry Kissinger)

DIAMOND Diamonds are nothing more than chunks of coal that stuck to their jobs. (Malcolm Forbes)

DIFFICULTY   It is not because things are difficult that we do not dare, it is because we do not dare that they are difficult. (Seneca)

DIFFICULTY   Real difficulties can be overcome, it is only the imaginary ones that are unconquerable. (TN Vail)

DIGITAL   Places don't matter to people any more. Places aren't the point. People are only ever half present where they are these days. They always have at least one foot in the great digital nowhere. (Matt Haig)

DIGNITY   You have got to learn to leave the table when love is no longer being served. (Nina Simone)

DIPLOMACY   All diplomacy is a continuation of war by other means. (Zhou Enlai)

DISCIPLINE   Discipline is the bridge between goals and accomplishment. (Jim Rohn)

DISCIPLINE   We must all suffer one of two things: the pain of discipline or the pain of regret or disappointment. (Jim Rohn)

DISEASE ☺ After you find out all the things that can go wrong, your life becomes less about living and more about waiting. (Chuck Palahniuk)

DISEASE ☺ First the doctor told me the good news : I was going to have a disease named after me. (Steve Martin)

DISRUPTION   A moment of disruption is where the conversation about disruption often begins, even though determining that moment is entirely hindsight. (Steven Sinofsky)

DIVORCE ☺   My divorce came to me as a complete surprise. That's what happens when you have not been home in eighteen years. (Lee Trevino)

DIVORCE ☺   My wife Mary and I have been married for forty-seven years and not once have we had an argument serious enough to consider divorce ; murder, yes, but divorce, never. (Jack Benny)

DIVORCE ☺   I am an excellent housekeeper. Every time I get a divorce, I keep the house. (ZZ Gabor)

DIVORCE ☺   My mother always sais don't marry for money, divorce for money. (Wendy Liebman)

DIVORCE ☺   She cried- and the judge wiped her tears with my checkbook. (Tommy Manville)

DIVORCE In every marriage more than a week old, there are grounds for divorce. The trick is to find, and continue to find, grounds for marriage. (Robert Anderson)

DOCTOR   In nothing do men more nearly approach the gods than in giving health to men. (Cicero)

DOCTOR Never go to a doctor whose office plants have died. (Erma Bombeck)

DOCTOR ☺ Doctors don't seem to realize that most of us are perfectly content not having to visualize ourselves as animated bags of skin filled with obscene glop. (Joe Haldeman)

DOCTOR ☺ Every patient is a doctor after his cure. (Irish proverb)

DOCTOR ☺ Finish last in your league and they call you idiot. Finish last in medical school and they call you doctor. (Abe Lamons)

DOCTOR ☺ I got the bill for my surgery. Now I know what those doctors were wearing masks for. (JH Boren)

DOCTOR   I got the bill for my surgery. Now I know what those doctors were wearing masks for. (JH Boren)

DOG   There is no psychiatrist in the world like a puppy licking your face. (Bern Williams)

DOG   You think dogs will not be in heaven? I tell you, they will be there long before any of us. (RL Stevenson)

DOG ☺   No one appreciates the very special genius of your conversation as the dog does. (C Morley)

DOG ☐   Whoever said you can't buy happiness forgot little puppies. (Gene Hill)

DOGS   Dogs are our link to paradise. They don't know evil or jealousy or discontent. To sit with a dog on a hillside on a glorious afternoon is to be back in Eden, where doing nothing was not boring- it was peace. (M Kundera)

DREAM   At first dreams seem impossible, then improbable, then inevitable. (Christopher Reeve)

DREAM   Don't be pushed by your problems, be led by your dreams. (RW Emerson)

DREAM   Having a dream you don't pursue is like buying an ice-cream cone and watching it melt all over your hand. (Frank Papasso)

DREAM   All that we see or seem is but a dream within a dream. (Edgar Allan Poe)

DREAM   Dreaming permits each and everyone of us to be quietly and safely insane every night of our lives". (William Dement)

DREAM   I was trying to daydream, but my mind kept wandering. (Steven Wright)

DREAM   It takes a lot of courage to show your dreams to someone else. (Erma Bombeck)

DREAM   Trust in dreams, for in them is hidden the gate to eternity. (Khalil Gibran)

DREAMS At first dreams seem impossible, then improbable, then inevitable. (Christopher Reeve)

DREAMS   Never let your memories be greater than your dreams. (Doug Ivester)

DRINKING ☺   My dad's a foster parent, whereas my mother has always preferred Carlsberg. (Tom Taylor)

DRINKING An intelligent man is sometimes forced to be drunk to spend time with his fools. (Ernest Hemingway)

DRIVING   The best car safety device is a rear-view mirror with a cop in it. (Dudley Moore)

DRUG ☺   I asked for a wake-up call at a hotel and they said, "You are a drug addict and you are killing yourself. (Andy Field)

DUPLICITYThe urge to save humanity is almost always a false face for the urge to rule it. (HL Mencken)

ECOMONY		In our economic structure, the people who work the hardest oftentimes make the least. (M Tubbs)

ECONOMICS		The purely economic man is indeed close to being a social moron. Economic theory has been much preoccupied with this rational fool. (RH Thaler)

ECONOMICS		Most economic fallacies derive from the tendency to assume that there is a fixed pie. (Milton Friedman)

ECONOMICS		The function of economic forecasting is to make astrology look respectable. (JK Galbraith)

ECONOMY Those who invented the law of supply and demand have no right to complain when the law works against their interest. (Anwar Sadat)

EDITOR		Newspaper editors are men who separate the wheat from the chaff, and then print the chaff. (A Stevenson)

EDUCATION		Education costs money. But so does ignorance. (Sir Claus Moser)

EDUCATION		Education is not preparation for life; education is life itself. (John Dewey)

EDUCATION		Education is the great engine of personal development. It is through education that the daughter of a peasant can become a doctor, that a son of a mineworker can become the head of the mine, that a child of farm workers can become president of a great nation. (Nelson Mandela)

EDUCATION   The end-product of education should be a free creative man, who can battle against historical circumstances and adversities of nature. (S Radhakrishnan)

EDUCATION   What sculpture is to a block of marble, education is to a human soul. (Joseph Addison)

EDUCATION   A university is just a group of buildings gathered around a library.(S Foote)

EDUCATION   A university is what a college becomes when the faculty loses interest in students. (John Ciardi)

EDUCATION   Education is simply the soul of a society as it passes from one generation to another. (GK Chesterton)

EDUCATION   Education is the ability to listen to almost anything without losing your temper or your self-confidence. (Robert Frost)

EDUCATION   I have never let my schooling interfere with my education. (Mark Twain)

EDUCATION   The roots of education are bitter, but the fruit is sweet. (Aristotle)

EDUCATION   When a subject becomes totally obsolete we make it a required course. (Peter Drucker)

EDUCATION   Educating the mind without educating the heart is no education at all. (Aristotle)

EDUCATION   Education is the ability to listen to almost anything without losing your temper or your self-confidence. (Robert Frost)

EDUCATION   From kindergarten onwards, we need education to strengthen inner values not just pursue material goals. We need to introduce emotional hygiene, much as we teach physical hygiene. This way we can address the problems we face, in the hope of making this a century of non-violence. (Dalai Lama)

EDUCATION   It will be a great day when our schools have all the money they need, and our air force has to have a bake-sale to buy a bomber. (Robert Fulghum)

EDUCATION   The best solution to income inequality is providing a high-quality education for everybody. In our highly technological, globalized economy, people without education will not be able to improve their economic situation. (Ben Bernanke)

EDUCATION   The philosophy of the school room in one generation will be the philosophy of government in the next. (Abraham Lincoln)

EFFORT   There are no traffic jams along the extra mile. (Roger Staubach)

EGO   Ego says, once everything falls into place, I'll feel peace. Spirit says, Find your peace, and then everything will fall into place. (Marianne Williamson)

EGO   The megalomaniac differs from the narcissist by the fact that he wishes to be powerful rather than charming, and seeks to be feared rather than loved. To this type belong many lunatics and most of the great men of history. (B Russell)

EGO   When a man is wrapped up in himself he makes a pretty small package. (John Ruskin)

ELECTION Any American who is prepared to run for president should automatically, by definition, be disqualified from ever doing so. (Gore Vidal)

ELECTION When I was a boy I was told that anybody could become President ; I am beginning to believe it. (Clarence Darrow)

EMBARRASSMENT		Embarrassment is a villain to be crushed. (R Cialdini)

EMOTION Even more important than knowledge is the life of emotion. The human race has survived hitherto owing to ignorance and incompetence, but given knowledge & competence combined with folly, there can be no certainly of survival. Knowledge will be increase of sorrow. (Bertrand Russell)

EMOTIONS		The degree of one's emotion varies inversely with one's knowledge of the facts – the less you know the hotter you get. (Bertrand Russell)

ENEMY	Pay attention to your enemies, for they are the first to discover your mistakes. (Antisthenes)

ENERGY		Instead of worrying about what you cannot control, shift your energy to what you can create. (RT Bennett)

ENERGY		The use of solar energy has not been opened up because the oil industry does not own the sun. (Ralph Nader)

ENERGY		What do oil company executives, vampires and NASA bureaucrats all have in common? They fear solar energy. (Michio Kaku)

ENTERPRISE		I could not find the sports car of my dreams, so I built it myself. (F Porsche)

ENTERPRISE   Behold the turtle. He only makes progress when he sticks his neck out. (James Bryant Conant)

ENTHUSIASM   Enthusiasm is the yeast that makes your hopes shine to the stars. (Henry Ford)

ENTHUSIASM   Enthusiasm is the master key to feeling great. It acts as a double energy boost. It keeps you positive and beyond the pull of negativity and also makes others feel good. Enthusiasm opens up a world of possibilities. (Dadi Janki)

ENTHUSIASM   Let a man lose everything else in the world but his enthusiasm and he will come through again. (H. W. Arnold)

ENVIRONMENT   Fire made us human, fossil fuels made us modern, but now we need a new fire that makes us safe, secure, healthy and durable. (Amory Lovins)

ENVIRONMENT   I think that I shall never see a billboard lovely as a tree. Indeed unless the billboards fall, I will never see a tree at all. (Ogden Nash)

ENVIRONMENT   Keep a green tree in your heart and perhaps a singing bird will come. (Chinese proverb)

ENVIRONMENT   Water and air, the two essential fluids on which all life depends, have become global garbage cans. (J Cousteau)

ENVY   Few of us can stand prosperity. Another man's, I mean. (Mark Twain)

ENVY   Moral indignation is jealousy with a halo. (HG Wells)

ESTATE ☺ When applying for a job as an estate agent, the interviewer worried that my CV was a bit small, I said actually it's really cozy and I was immediately hired. (Alex Kealy)

ETHICS   Ethics is the activity of man directed to secure the inner perfection of his own personality. (Albert Schweitzer)

ETHICS ☺ Relativity applies to physics, not ethics. (Albert Einstein)

ETIQUETTE   All etiquette (and diplomacy is nothing but a lot of) hot air. But that is what is in our automobile tires, notice how it eases the bumps. (Georges Clemenceau)

EVIL   While choosing between two evils, I always like to try the one I have never tried before. (Mae West)

EXAMPLE A good example is the best sermon. (B Franklin)

EXCELLENCE   I am careful not to confuse excellence with perfection. Excellence I can reach for, perfection is God's business. (Michael Fox)

EXCELLENCE   It is so much worse to be a mediocre artist than to be a mediocre post-office clerk. (Rudolf Bing)

EXCELLENCE   Nobody who ever gave their best regretted it. (George Halas)

EXCELLENCE   People forget how fast you did a job, but they remember how well you did it. (Howard W. Newton)

EXCELLENCE   Perfection is not attainable. But if we chase perfection, we can catch excellence.

EXERCISE I don't count my sit-ups; I only start counting when it starts hurting because they're the only ones that count. (Muhammed Ali)

EXPERIENCE   Experience is not what happens to you, it's what you do with what happens to you. (Aldous Huxley)

EXPERIENCE   In the business world, everyone is paid in two coins : cash and experience. Take the experience first ; the cash will come later. (Harold Geneen)

EXPERIENCE   We learn from experience. A man never wakes up his second baby just to see it smile. (Grace Williams)

EXPERTISE   The man we call a specialist today was formerly called a man with a one-track mind. (Endre Balogh)

FACEBOOK   If you want to understand the difference between a network and a community, ask your Facebook friends to help paint your house. (Henry Minztberg)

FACT   All generalizations are false, including this one. (Mark Twain)

FACT   Facts do not cease to exist because they are ignored. (AL Huxley)

FACT   I would rather be vaguely right than precisely wrong. (JM Keynes)

FACT   Value judgements are not to be established on the basis of facts- and that is a fact. (JW Krutch)

FAILURE   Failure is a trickster with a keen sense of irony and cunning. It takes great delight in tripping one when success is almost within reach. (N Hill)

FAILURE   Failure should be our teacher, not our undertaker. Failure is delay, not defeat. It is a temporary detour, not a dead end. Failure is something we can avoid only by saying nothing, doing nothing, and being nothing. (Denis Waitley)

FAILURE   I cannot give you the formula for success, but I can give you the formula for failure which is : Try to please everybody. (HB Swope)

FAILURE   I think failure is nothing more than life's way of nudging you that you are off course. (Sara Blakely)

FAILURE   Make failure your teacher, not your undertaker. (Zig Ziglar)

FAILURE   Only those who dare to fail greatly can ever achieve greatly. (RF Kennedy)

FAILURE   Sometimes not getting what you want is a wonderful stroke of luck. (Dalai Lama)

FAILURE   Take chances, make mistakes. That is how you grow. Pain nourishes your courage. You have to fail in order to practice being brave. (Mary Tyler Moore)

FAILURE   You build on failure. You use it as a stepping stone. Close the door on the past. You don't try to forget the mistakes, but you don't dwell on it. You don't let it have any of your energy, or any of your time, or any of your space. (J Cash)

FAILURE   Failure is a feeling long before it is an actual result. (Michelle Obama)

FAILURE   Failure is the condiment that gives success its flavor. (Truman Capote)

FAILURE   He was a self-made man who owed his lack of success to nobody. (Joseph Heller)

FAILURE   I have failed many times, but I have never gone into a game expecting myself to fail. (Michael Jordan)

FAILURE   If things go wrong, don't go with them. (Roger Babson)

FAILURE   No experiment is ever a complete failure. It can always be used as a bad example. (P.Dickson)

FAILURE   We need to accept that we won't always make the right decisions, that we will screw up royally sometimes- understanding that failure is not the opposite of success, it is part of success. (Arianna Huffington)

FAILURE   You may have a fresh start any moment you choose, for this thing that we call failure is not the falling down, but the staying down. (Mary Pickford)

FAITH   Sometimes your only available transportation is a leap of faith. (Margaret Shepherd)

FAITH   As your faith is strengthened you will find that there is no longer the need to have a sense of control, and that things will ow as they will, and that you will flow with them, to your great delight and benefit. (Emmanuel Teney)

FAITH   Faith is taking the first step even when you don't see the whole staircase. (Martin Luther King, Jr)

FAITH   Faith makes many of the mountains which it has to remove. (Dean WR Inge)

FAITH   Fear can keep us up all night long, but faith makes one fine pillow. (Philip Gulley)

FAITH   The smallest seed of faith is better than the largest fruit of happiness. (HD Thoreau)

FAME   If you have earned a position, be proud of it. Don't hide it. I want to be recognized. When I hear people say, There's Joan Crawford ! I turn around and say, Hi, How are you? (Joan Crawford)

FAME   Fame means millions of people have the wrong idea of who you are. (Erica Jong)

FAME   I like being famous when it's convenient for me and completely anonymous when it's not. (C Deneuve)

FAME   No man, however great, is known to everybody and no man, however solitary, is known to nobody. (Thomas Moore)

FAME   Wealth is like sea-water ; the more we drink, the thirstier we become ; and the same is true of fame. (Arthur Schopenhauer)

FAMILY   All happy families are alike, each unhappy family is unhappy in its own way. (Leo Tolstoy)

FAMILY   Basically, I believe the world is a jungle, and if it is not a bit of a jungle in the home, a child cannot possibly be fit to enter the outside world. (Bette Davis)

FAMILY   By the time a man realizes that maybe his father was right, he usually has a son who thinks he's wrong. - Charles Wadsworth

FAMILY   Happiness is having a large, loving, caring, close-knit family in another city. (George Burns)

FAMILY   The proper time to influence the character of a child is about a hundred years before he is born. (John Adams)

FANATICISM   Fanaticism consists in redoubling your efforts when you have forgotten your aim. (George Santayana)

FAREWELL   Goodbyes are only for those who love with their eyes. Because for those who love with heart and soul there is no such thing as separation. (Rumi)

FASHION   Had a look at the alligators. Just floating handbags, really. (Trevor Griffiths)

FASHION Every generation laughs at the old fashions, but follows religiously the new. (HD Thoreau)

FEAR   Fear makes the wolf bigger than he is. (German proverb)

FEMINISM   We are the women our parents warned us against, and we are proud. (Gloria Steinem)

FEMINISM ☺   There are really not many jobs that actually require a penis or a vagina, and all other occupations should be open to everyone. (Gloria Steinem)

FILMS   A good film is when the price of the dinner, the theatre admission and the babysitter were worth it. (Alfred Hitchcock)

FLATTERY Apparently we have such an automatically positive reaction to compliments that we can fall victim to someone who uses them in an obvious attempt to win our favor. (Robert Cialdini)

FLATTERY There is no other way to guard yourself against flattery than by making men understand that telling you the truth will not offend you. (Niccolò Machiavelli)

FLOWER ☺Send me flowers while I am alive. They won't do me a damn bit of good when I am dead. (Joan Crawford)

FOCUS   I fear not the man who has practiced 10,000 kicks once, but I fear the man who had practiced one kick 10,000 times. (Bruce Lee)

FOCUS   The successful warrior is the average man, with laser-like focus. (Bruce Lee)

FOCUS   Concentrate all your thoughts upon the work at hand. The sun's rays do not burn until brought to a focus. (Alexander G Bell)

FOCUS   You can't depend on your eyes when your imagination is out of focus. (Mark Twain)

FOCUS   The joy we feel has little to do with the circumstances of our lives and everything to do with the focus of our lives. (RM Nelson)

FOOL   A fool flatters himself, a wise man flatters the fool. (EG Bulwer-Lytton)

FOOL   The cleverest of all, in my opinion, is the man who calls himself a fool at least once a month. (Fyodor Dostoevsky)

FOOL   A common mistake that people make when trying to design something completely foolproof is to underestimate the ingenuity of complete fools. (Douglas Adams)

FOOL   Every man is a damn fool for at least five minutes every day, wisdom consists of not exceeding the limit. (Elbert Hubbard)

FOOL   I have great faith in fools, self-confidence my friends   call   it.
(Edgar Allan Poe)

FOOL   There are two ways to be fooled. One is to believe what isn't true, the other is to refuse to believe what is true. (Søren Kierkegaard)

FOOTBALL ☺   Some people believe football is a matter of life and death. I am very disappointed with that attitude. I can assure you it is much, much more important than that. (Bill Shankley)

FOOTBALL If a man watches three football games in a row, he should be declared legally dead. (Erma Bombeck)

FORGIVENESS   Forgiveness liberates the soul. It removes fear. That is why it is such a powerful weapon. (Nelson Mandela)

FORGIVENESS   If you ever get the chance to treat them the way they treated you, I hope you choose to walk away and do better. (Najwa Zebian)

FORGIVENESS   Forgive people, move on and let them continue with their lives. You are moving into a direction that they are not mentally prepared for. DOn't disrupt the universe's plan. (Megan Roxanne)

FORGIVENESS   Forgiveness is like this : A room can be dark because you have closed the windows and curtains. But the sun is shining outside. You have to get up and open the window and draw the curtains apart to let in the sunlight and fresh air. (Desmond Tutu)

FORGIVENESS   Forgiveness is not always easy. At times, it feels more painful than the wound we suffered, to forgive the one that inflicted it. And yet, there is no peace without forgiveness. (M Williamson)

FORGIVENESS Forgiveness liberates the soul. It removes fear. That is why it is such a powerful weapon. (Nelson Mandela)

FORGIVENESS   If you ever get the chance to treat them the way they treated you, I hope you choose to walk away and do better. (Najwa Zebian)

FORTITUDE   Fortitude is the capacity to say no when the world wants to hear yes. (Erich Fromm)

FRAUD   Fraud is the daughter of greed. (Jonathan Gash)

FRAUD   Bankruptcy is a legal proceeding in which you put your money in your pants pocket and give your coat to your creditors. (Joey Adams)

FREEDOM Freedom is not worth having if it does not include the freedom to make mistakes (MK Gandhi)

FREEDOM Freedom is the right to tell people what they do not want to hear. (George Orwell)

FREEDOM He was jeopardizing his traditional rights of freedom and independence by daring to exercise them. (Joseph Heller)

FREEDOM If the freedom of speech is taken away then dumb and silent we may be led , like sheep to the slaughter. (George Washington)

FREEDOM If we don't believe in freedom of expression for people we despise, we don't believe in it at all. (Noam Chomsky)

FREEDOM It is by the goodness of God that in our country we have those three unspeakably precious things : freedom of speech, freedom of conscience, and the prudence never to practice either of them. (Mark Twain)

FORGIVENESS Forgiveness liberates the soul. It removes fear. That is why it is such a powerful weapon. (Nelson Mandela)

FORGIVENESS If you ever get the chance to treat them the way they treated you, I hope you choose to walk away and do better. (Najwa Zebian)

FRIEND Anybody can sympathise with the sufferings of a friend, but it requires a very fine nature to sympathise with a friend's success. (Oscar Wilde)

FRIEND Friendship is everything. Friendship is more than talent. It is more than the government. It is almost the equal of family. (Mario Puzo)

FRIEND Friendship is unnecessary, like philosophy, like art...It has no survival value ; rather it is one of those things which give value to survival. (CS Lewis)

FRIEND I don't need a friend who changes when I change and who nods when I nod ; my shadow does that much better. (Plutarch)

FRIEND It is not so much our friend's help that helps us, as the confidence of their help. (Epicurus)

FRIEND Men kick friendship around like a football but it does not seem to break. Women treat it like glass and it goes to pieces. (AM Lindbergh)

FRIEND The language of friendship is not words but meanings. (HD Thoreau)

FRIEND   The proper office of a friend is to side with you when you are wrong. Nearly anybody will side with you when you are right. (Mark Twain)

FRIEND   To throw away an honest friend is, as it were, to throw your life away. (Sophocles)

FRIEND   When someone tells you the truth, lets you think for yourself, experience your own emotions, he is treating you as a true equal. As a friend. (Whitney Otto)

FRIEND ☺ I tell my friends I am here for them 24/7 because it sounds better than saying, I am only here for them on 24 July. (Andy Field)

FRIEND ☺ The capacity for friendship is God's way of apologizing for our families. (Jay McInerney)

FRIEND   A doubtful friend is worse than a certain enemy. Let a man be one thing or the other, and we then know how to meet him. (Aesop)

FRIEND   Do not use a hatchet to remove a fly from your friend's forehead. (Chinese proverb)

FRIEND   He is a fine friend. He stabs you in the front (LL Levinson)

FRIENDSHIP   A friend should always underestimate your virtues and an enemy overestimate your faults. (Mario Puzo)

FRIENDSHIP   Friendship is everything. Friendship is more than talent. It is more than the government. It is almost the equal of family. (Mario Puzo)

FRIENDSHIP   Look at your 5 closest friends. Those 5 friends are who you are. If you don't like who you are then you know what you have to do. (Will Smith)

FUN   To love what you do and feel that it matters-
how could anything be more fun? (Katherine Graham)

FUTURE   You can only predict things after they
have happened. (E Ionesco)

GANDHI   If humanity is to progress, Gandhi is
inescapable. He lived, thought and acted, inspired by the
vision of humanity evolving toward a world of peace and
harmony. We may ignore him at our own risk. (ML King
Jr.)

GENIUS   Men of genius are often dull and inert in
society ; as the blazing meteor, when it descends to earth,
is only a stone. (Henry Longfellow)

GENIUS   No great genius has ever existed without
some touch of madness. (Aristotle)

GENIUS   Talent hits a target no one else can hit ;
Genius hits a target no one else can see. (Arthur
Schopenhauer)

GENIUS   The public is wonderfully tolerant. It forgives
everything except genius. (Oscar Wilde)

GENIUS ☺ There is a fine line between genius and
insanity. I have erased this line. (Oscar Levant)

GENIUS   In every work of genius we recognize
our own rejected thoughts, they come back to us with a
certain alienated majesty. (RW Emerson)

GENIUS   There is no genius free from some
tincture of madness. (Seneca)

GIVING   We often live as if our happiness depended on
having. But true joy and inner peace come from giving of
ourselves to others. A happy life is a life for others. That

truth, is usually discovered when we are confronted with our brokenness. (Henri Nouwen)

GOAL   Celebrate what you have accomplished, but also raise the bar a little higher each time you succeed. (Mia Hamm)

GOAL   A goal should scare you a little, and excite you a lot. (Joe Vitale)

GOAL   All my life I wanted to be somebody. Now I see that I should have been more specific. (Jane Wagner)

GOAL   Efforts and courage are not enough without purpose and direction. (John F. Kennedy)

GOAL   If people are not laughing at your goals, your goals are too small. (Azim Premji)

GOAL   If you don't know where you are going, any road will get you there. (Lewis Carroll)

GOAL   It is a paradoxical but profoundly true and important principle of life that the most likely way to reach a goal is to be aiming not at that goal itself but at some more ambitious goal beyond it. (Arnold Joseph Toynbee)

GOAL   The first step to getting the things you want out of life is this. Decide what you want. (Ben Stein)

GOD   I believe God is managing affairs and that He does not need any advice from me. With God in charge, I believe everything will work out for the best in the end. So, what is there to worry about. (Henry Ford)

GOD   God is a comedian playing to an audience too afraid to laugh. (Voltaire)

GOD ☺   I fear one day I'll meet God, he'll sneeze and I won't know what to say. (Ronnie Shakes)

GOD	God is not a cosmic bell-boy. (HE Fosdick)

GOODNESS	Waste no more time arguing about what a good man should be. Be one. (Marcus Aurelius)

GOODNESS	Be good and you will be lonesome. (Mark Twain)

GOODNESS	Do your little bit of good where you are, it is those little bits of good put together that overwhelm the world. (Desmond Tutu)

GOODNESS	People don't notice goodness because it is transparent like water and air, only if it runs out, does it become noticeable. (Laszlo Nemeth)

GOODNESS	There is nothing so nice as doing good by stealth and being found out by accident. (Charles Lamb)

GOSSIP	The last to learn of gossip are the parties concerned. (Khushwant Singh)

GOVERNANCE	He that would govern others first should be the master of himself. (Philip M)

GOVERNANCE	The poor object to being governed badly, while the rich object to being governed at all. (GK Chesterton)

GOVERNMENT	We have the best government that money can buy. (Mark Twain)

GOVERNMENT ☺ Be thankful we are not getting all the government we are paying for. (Will Rogers)

GOVERNMENT ☺ If you put the federal government in charge of the Sahara desert, in 5 years there would be a shortage of sand. (Milton Friedman)

GOVERNMENT   A nation of sheep will beget a government of wolves. (Edward R Murrow)

GOVERNMENT   Government does not solve problems ; it subsidizes them. (Ronald Reagan)

GOVERNMENT   The best government is a benevolent tyranny tempered by an occasional assassination. (Voltaire)

GRATEFUL   Be grateful for whoever comes, because each has been sent as a guide from beyond. (Rumi)

GRATEFUL ☺   The only people with whom you should try to get even are those who have helped you. (JE Southard)

GRATEFULNESS   When eating fruit, think of the person who planted the tree. (Vietnamese proverb)

GRATITIDE   Gratitude makes sense of the past, brings peace for today, and creates a vision for tomorrow. (Melody Beattie)

GRATITUDE   Not what we say about our blessings, but how we use them, is the true measure of our thanksgiving. (Purkiser)

GRATITUDE   Gratitude unlocks the fullness of life. It turns what we have into enough. (Melody Beattie)

GRATITUDE   Let gratitude be the pillow upon which you kneel to say your nightly prayer. (Maya Angelou)

GROWTH Everyone wants to live on top of the mountain, but all the happiness and growth occurs while you are climbing it. (Andy Rooney)

GROWTH   Growth for the sake of growth is the ideology of the cancer cell. (Edward Abbey)

HABIT   The older generation thought nothing of getting up at five every morning – and the younger generation does not think much of it either. (JJ Welsh)

HABIT   Men's natures are alike; it is their habits that separate them.   (Confucius)

HABIT   The chains of habit are too weak to be felt until they are too strong to be broken. (Samuel Johnson)

HAIR ☺   I think that the most important thing a woman can have-next to talent, of course- is her hairdresser. (Joan Crawford)

HAPPINESS   A happy person is not a person in a certain set of circumstances, but rather a person with a certain set of attitudes. (Hugh Downs)

HAPPINESS   Happiness can exist only in acceptance. (George Orwell)

HAPPINESS   Happiness cannot be travelled to, owned, earned, worn or consumed. Happiness is the spiritual experience of living every minute with love, grace, and gratitude. (Denis Waitley)

HAPPINESS   Happiness is a choice that requires effort at times. (Aeschylus)

HAPPINESS   Happiness is a warm puppy. (C Schulz)

HAPPINESS   Happiness is an attitude. We either make ourselves miserable, or happy and strong. The amount of work is the same. (F Reigler)

HAPPINESS   Happiness is that state of consciousness which proceeds from the achievement of one's values. (Ayn Rand)

HAPPINESS   If what Proust says is true, that happiness is the absence of fever, then I will never know happiness. For I am possessed by a fever for knowledge, experience, and creation. (A Nin)

HAPPINESS   If you have not taken the time to define what happiness means to you, what have you spent your whole life Pursuing? (Bo Bennett)

HAPPINESS   My guru says that people universally tend to think that happiness is a stroke of luck, something that will maybe descend upon you like fine weather if you are fortunate enough. But that is not how happiness works, Happiness is the consequence of personal effort. (E Gilbert)

HAPPINESS   No one has a right to consume happiness without producing it. (Helen Keller)

HAPPINESS   Nothing captures the biological argument better than the famous New Age slogan: 'Happiness begins within.' Money, social status, plastic surgery, beautiful houses, powerful positions – none of these will bring you happiness. Lasting happiness comes only from serotonin, dopamine and oxytocin. (YN Harari)

HAPPINESS   On the highway of life, we most often recognize happiness out of the rear view mirror. (Frank Tyger)

HAPPINESS   Pleasure may come from illusion, but happiness can come only of reality. (Chamfort)

HAPPINESS   The art of living does not consist in preserving and clinging to a particular mood of happiness, but in allowing happiness to change its form without being disappointed by the change, for happiness, like a child, must be allowed to grow up. (Charles Morgan)

HAPPINESS   The easiest way to increase happiness is to control your use of time. Can you find more time to do the things you enjoy doing?" – Daniel Kahneman

HAPPINESS   The first recipe for happiness is : Avoid too lengthy meditation on the past. (Andre Maurois)

HAPPINESS   The happiness of life is made up of the little charities of a kiss or smile, a kind look, a heartfelt compliment. (ST Coleridge)

HAPPINESS   The secret of happiness is to count your blessings while others are adding up their troubles. (William Penn)

HAPPINESS   The word 'happiness' would lose its meaning if it were not balanced by sadness. (Carl Jung)

HAPPINESS   There can be no happiness if the things we believe in are different from the things we do. (Freya Stark)

HAPPINESS   They say a person needs just three things to be truly happy in this world : someone to love, something to do, and something to hope for. (Tom Bodett)

HAPPINESS   They say it is better to be poor and happy than rich and miserable, but how about a compromise like moderately rich and just moody? (Princess Diana)

HAPPINESS   When I was 5 years old, my mom always told me that happiness was the key to life. When I went to school, they asked me what I wanted to do when I grow up. I wrote down "happy". They told me I did not understand the assignment and I told them they did not understand life. (John Lennon)

HAPPINESS ☺   If you wish to be happy yourself, you must resign yourself to seeing others also happy. (Bertrand Russell)

HAPPINESS   Most people are about as happy as they make up their minds to be. (Abraham Lincoln)

HAPPINESS   Sometimes happiness quietly curls up in your heart just to snuggle. (Richelle E. Goodrich)

HAPPINESS   The search for happiness is one of the chief sources of unhappiness. (Eric Hoffer)

HAPPINESS   A sincere, balanced and kind attitude towards ourselves as well as others is the key to happiness and success in life's all avenues. (Janos Selye)

HAPPINESS   And there is even a happiness, that makes the heart afraid. (Thomas Hood)

HAPPINESS   Be happy in the moment, that's enough. Each moment is all we need, not more. (Mother Teresa)

HAPPINESS   Be pleasant until ten o'clock in the morning and the rest of the day will take care of itself. (Elbert Hubbard)

HAPPINESS   Happiness is not being pained in body or troubled in mind. (Thomas Jefferson)

HAPPINESS   Happiness makes up in height for what it lacks in length. (Robert Frost)

HAPPINESS   Happy the man who early learns the wide chasm that lies between his wishes and his powers. (Goethe)

HAPPINESS   I am a kind of paranoid in reverse. I suspect people of plotting to make my happy. (JD Salinger)

HAPPINESS   If you want to be happy, set a goal that commands your thoughts, liberates your energy & inspires your hopes. (A. Carnegie)

HAPPINESS   Most of us believe in trying to make other people happy only if they can be happy in ways which we approve. (RS Lynd)

HAPPINESS   Sanity and happiness are an impossible combination. (Mark Twain)

HAPPINESS   The first requisite for the happiness of the people is the abolition of religion. (Karl Marx)

HARDWORK   Do your future self a favour and work hard now. (J Cole)

HATE ☺   I told my psychiatrist that everyone hates me. He said I was being ridiculous- everyone has not met me yet. (Rodney Dangerfield)

HATE   Hating people is like burning down your own house to get rid of a rat. (HE Fosdick)

HATE   Hatred is the coward's revenge for being intimidated. (GB Shaw)

HEALING   Energy healing is like defragmenting your hard drive. The scattered pieces of yourself become whole again. (JR Payette)

HEALTH   The six best doctors in the world are sunlight, rest, exercise, diet, self-confidence, and friends. Maintain them in all stages and enjoy a healthy life. (Steve Jobs)

HEALTH   Medical Science has made such tremendous progress that there is hardly a healthy human left. (Aldous Huxley)

HEALTH   A lot of people are afraid of heights. Not me, I am afraid of widths. (Steven Wright)

HEART   The funny thing about the heart is a soft heart is a strong heart, and a hard heart is a weak heart. (Criss Jami)

HEART   I know that ultimately one is guided not by the intellect but by the heart. The heart accepts a conclusion for which the intellect subsequently finds reasoning. Argument follows conviction. Man often finds reason in support of whatever he does or wants to do. (M.Gandhi)

HEART   When the heart speaks, the mind finds it indecent to object. (Milan Kundera)

HEART   It takes very little to fill up a big heart. (Antonio Porchia)

HEART   The heart has its reasons which reason does not understand. (Rochefoucauld)

HERO   We do not have to become heroes overnight. Just a step at a time, meeting each thing that comes up... discovering we have strength to stare it down. (Eleanor Roosevelt)

HERO   Show me a hero and I will write you a tragedy. (FS Fitzgerald)

HERO	We can't all be heroes because someone has to sit on the curb and clap as they go by. (Will Rogers)

HEROISM	True heroism is remarkably sober, very undramatic. It is not the urge to surpass all others at whatever cost, but the urge to serve others at whatever cost. (Arthur Ashe)

HISTORY History is hereditary only in this way: we, all of us, inherit everything, and then we choose what to cherish, what to disavow, and what do do next, which is why it's worth trying to know where things come from. (Jill Lepore)

HISTORY ☺	History will be kind to me, for I intend to write it. (Winston Churchill)

HISTORY	Any event, once it has occurred, can be made to appear inevitable by a competent historian. (Lee Simonson)

HISTORY	History is a cyclic poem written by Time upon the memories of man. (PB Shelley)

HISTORY	History is a pact between the dead, the living, and the yet unborn. (Edmund Burke)

HISTORY	History is the discovering of the constant and universal principles of human nature. (David Hume)

HISTORY	History is the record of an encounter between character and circumstance. (Donald Creghton)

HISTORY	Not to know the events which happened before one was born, that is to remain always a boy. (Cicero)

HISTORY	We learn from history that we do not learn from history.(Georg Hegel)

HOARDING   Keep a thing for seven years and you will find use for it. (Irish proverb)

HOME   A man travels the whole world over in search of what he needs and returns home to find it. (GA Moore)

HOME   Decorate your home. It gives the illusion that your life is more interesting than it really is. (Charles M Schulz)

HOME   Home is where you can say anything you please, because nobody pays any attention to you anyway. (Joe Moore)

HOMEMAKER   The homemaker has the ultimate career. All other careers exist for one purpose only – and that is to support the ultimate career.(C.S. Lewis)

HONESTY A commentary on the times is that the word 'honesty' is now preceded by 'old-fashioned. (Larry Wolters)

HONESTY Honesty without compassion and understanding is not honesty, but subtle hostility. (Dr. R.N. Franzblau)

HONESTY It is easier to be dishonest for two than for one. (John Fowles)

HONESTY There is one way to find out if a man is honest – ask him, if he says, 'Yes', you know he is a crook. (Groucho Marx)

HOPE   Hope is like a road in the country; there was never a road, but when many people walk on it, the road comes into existence. (Lyn Yutang)

HOPE   In the depth of winter, I finally learned that within me there lay an invincible summer. (Albert Camus)

HOPE   The very least you can do in your life is to figure out what you hope for. And the most you can do is live inside that hope. (Barbara Kingsolver)

HOPE   Hope is the thing with feathers that perches in the soul- and sings the tunes without the words- and never stops at all. (Emily Dickinson)

HOPE   For myself I am an optimist – it does not seem to be much use to be anything else. (Winston S. Churchill)

HOPE   How deceitful hope may be, yet she carries us on pleasantly to the end of life. (Rochefoucauld)

HOPE   There is no medicine like hope, no incentive so great, and no tonic so powerful as expectation of something tomorrow. (OS Marden)

HOPE   We hope vaguely, but dread precisely. (Paul Valery)

HOSPITAL In the sick room, ten cents' worth of human understanding equals ten dollars' worth of medical science. (Martin H. Fischer)

HOSPITAL ☺   A hospital should also have a recovery room adjoining the cashier's office. (Francis O'Walsh)

HOSPITAL A hospital bed is a parked taxi with the meter running. (Groucho Marx)

HOSPITAL A hospital should also have a recovery room adjoining the cashier's office. (Francis O'Walsh)

HUG ☺   Oh, I love hugging. I wish I was an octopus, so I could hug 10 people at a time! (Drew Barrymore)

HUMANITY   You must not lose faith in humanity. Humanity is an ocean, if a few drops of the ocean are dirty, the ocean does not become dirty. (MK Gandhi)

HUMILITY Humility is about refusing to get all tangled up with yourself. It is about surrender, receptivity, awareness, simplicity. Breathing in. Breathing out. (Cheryl Strayed)

HUMILITY Humility is not renunciation of pride but the substitution of one pride for another. (Eric Hoffer)

HUMILITY Humility makes great men twice honorable. (Benjamin Franklin)

HUMILITY They are proud in humility, proud in that they are not proud. (Robert Burton)

HUMILITY True humility is not thinking less of yourself, it is thinking of yourself less. (CS Lewis)

HUMILITY When you win, say nothing. When you lose, say less. (Paul Brown)

HUMOUR Humor is the antidote to overthinking. It's a way of saying that life is paradoxical. Humor contains contradictions; it does not resolve them but revels in them. It says that the right way to exist among the contradictions, paradoxes, and absurdities of life is to cope with them through laughter.(Bob Mankoff)

HUNGER   No one can worship God or love his neighbour on an empty stomach. (Woodrow Wilson)

HUSBAND ☺   The husband who decides to surprise his wife is often very much surprised himself. (Voltaire)

HYPOCRICY   Some folks can look so busy doing nothing that they seem indispensable. (Kin Hubbard)

HYPOCRISY   If it were not for the intellectual snobs who pay, the arts would perish with their starving practitioners- let us thank heaven for hypocrisy. (Aldous Huxley)

IDEA   There is zero correlation between being the best talker and having the best ideas. (Susan Cain)

IDEA   An idea that is not dangerous is unworthy of being called an idea at all. (Oscar Wilde)

IDEA   I can't understand why people are frightened of new ideas. I'm frightened of the old ones. (John Cage)

IDEA   Take up one idea. Make that one idea your life- think of it, dream of it, live on that idea. Let the brain, muscles, nerves, every part of your body be full of that idea, and just leave every other idea alone. This is the way to success. (Swami Vivekananda)

IDEA   There is one thing stronger than all the armies in the world : and that is an idea whose time has come. (Victor Hugo)

IDEALIST   An idealist is one who, on noticing that a rose smells better than a cabbage, concludes that it will also make better soup. (HL Mencken)

IDEALIST   Every dogma has its day, but ideals are eternal. (I Zangwill)

IDEALIST   Idealism increases in direct proportion to one's distance from the problem. (J Galsworthy)

IDEALIST   The instinctive need to be the member of a closely knit group fighting for common ideals may grow so strong that it becomes inessential what these ideals are. (K Lorenz)

IDENTITY Do not free a camel of the burden of his hump; you may be freeing him from being a camel. (GK Chesterton)

IDENTITY I never wanted to be the next Bruce Lee. I just wanted to be the first Jackie Chan. (Jackie Chan)

IDENTITY To be nobody but yourself in a world which is doing its best, night and day, to make you everybody else means to fight the hardest battle which any human being can fight, and never stop fighting. (EE Cummings)

IDENTITY A nickname is the hardest stone that the devil can throw at a man. (W Hazlitt)

IDLENESS It is impossible to enjoy idling thoroughly unless one has plenty of work to do. There is no fun in doing nothing when you have nothing to do. Wasting time is merely an occupation then, and a most exhausting one. Idleness, like kiss, to be sweet, must be stolen. (Jerome K Jerome)

IGNORANCE   When I cannot brag about knowing something, I brag about not knowing it. (RW Emerson)

IGNORANCE   Gross ignorance : 144 times worse than ordinary ignorance. (Bennett Cerf)

IGNORANCE   One part of knowledge consists in being ignorant of such things as are not worthy to be known. (Crates)

IMAGE   If you celebrate your differentness, the world will, too. It believes exactly what you tell it—

through the words you use to describe yourself, the actions you take to care for yourself, and the choices you make to express yourself. (Victoria Moran)

IMAGE   In the end, it is impossible not to become what others believe you are. (Caesar)

IMAGE   There can be no true friends without true enemies. Unless we hate what we are not, we cannot love what we are. (Samuel P. Huntington)

IMAGE   Now when I bore people at a party, they think it's their fault. (Henry Kissinger)

IMAGE   Reputation is a bubble which bursts when a man tries to blow it up for himself. (Emma Carleton)

IMAGE   Who has once the fame to be an early riser may sleep till noon. (James Howell)

IMAGE   Your reputation is what others are not thinking about you. (Tom Masson)

IMAGINATION   The power of imagination makes us infinite. (John Muir)

IMAGINATION   This world is but a canvas to our imagination. (HD Thoreau)

IMPORVISATION Though nobody can go back and make a new beginning... Anyone can start over and make a new ending. (Chico Xavier)

IMPROVISATION Stay committed to your decisions, but stay flexible in your approach. (Tony Robbins)

INDECISION   He who hesitates gets bumped from the rear. (Homer Phillips)

INDECISION   I don't know what to do. My heart says yes, my mind says no, and I have not heard my liver yet. (Leopold Fechtner)

INDECISION   Some persons are very decisive when it comes to avoiding decisions. ((Brendan Francis)

INDECISION   I will give you a definite maybe. (Samuel Goldwyn)

INDIFFERENCE   The worst sin towards our fellow creatures is not to hate them, but to be indifferent to them, that is the essence of inhumanity. (GB Shaw)

INEQUALITY   The worst form of inequality is to try to make unequal things equal. (Aristotle)

INFINITY Burn worldly love, rub the ashes and make ink of it, make the heart the pen, the intellect the writer, write that which has no end or limit. (Guru Nanak)

INFLUENCE   The secret of my influence has always been that it remained secret. (Salvador Dali)

INFORMATION   In the information society, nobody thinks. We expected to banish paper, but we actually banished thought. (Michael Crichton)

INJURY   Reject your sense of injury and the injury itself disappears. (Marcus Aurelius)

INJUSTICE   Cry. Forgive. Learn. Move on. Let your tears water the seeds of your future happiness. (Steve Maraboli)

INNOVATION   Creativity is an input to innovation and the change is the output from innovation. (B Kelley)

INNOVATION   Expertise is the enemy of innovation. (Stephen Shapiro)

INNOVATION   There is a phrase in Buddhism , 'Beginner's mind'. It is wonderful to have a beginner's mind. (Steve Jobs)

INNOVATION   If I had asked people what they wanted, they would have said faster horses. (Henry Ford)

INSANITY In individuals, insanity is rare ; but in groups, parties, nations and epochs, it is the rule. (Nietzsche)

INSANITY There nearly always is method in madness. It is what drives men mad, being methodical. (GK Chesterton)

INSANITY We cannot unthink unless we are insane. (Arthur Koestler)

INSOMNIAC   Only by recalling a dream is an insomniac sure he has slept. (Mo Van)

INSTITUTION   Every great institution is the lengthened shadow of a single man. (Thomas Edison)

INSTITUTION   We all make the mistake of thinking about institutions, such as business, and government, as ends in themselves. (Adali Stevenson)

INSTITUTIONS   A fortress does not fall unless its towers are weakened. (SR Crawford)

INSULT   For you to insult me, I must first value your opinion. (Joubert Botha)

INSURANCE   There are worse things in life than death. Have you ever spent an evening with an insurance salesman? (Woody Allen)

INTEGRITY   Integrity is telling myself the truth. And honesty is telling the truth to other people. (Spencer Johnson)

INTEGRITY   Somebody once said that in looking for people to hire, you look for three qualities- integrity, intelligence and energy. And if they don't have the first, the other two will kill you. You think about it, it's true. If you hire somebody without the first, you really want them dumb and lazy. (Warren Buffet)

INTEGRITY   Take integrity over popularity and you will always be cool. (Carlos Santana)

INTEGRITY   The more cashless our society becomes, the more our moral compass slips. (Dan Ariely)

INTELLECT   And certainly we should take care not to make the intellect our god, it has, of course powerful muscles but no personality. It cannot lead, it can only serve, and it is not fastidious about its choice of leader. The intellect has a sharp eye for methods and tools, but it is blind to ends and values. (Einstein)

INTELLECT   The intellect is blind and cannot move of itself-it is an inactive, secondary help, the real help is feeling, love. Intellect is like limbs without the power of locomotion. It is only when feeling enters and gives them motion that they move and work on others. It is the heart that takes one to the highest place, which intellect can never reach. It goes beyond intellect and reaches what is called inspiration. (Swami Vivekananda)

INTELLIGENCE   Intellect distinguishes between the possible and the impossible ; reason distinguishes between the sensible and the senseless. Even the possible can be senseless. (Max Born)

INTELLIGENCE   The voice of the intelligence is drowned out by the roar of fear. It is ignored by the voice of desire. It is contradicted by the voice of shame. It is biased by hate and extinguished by anger. Most of all it is silenced by ignorance. (Karl A. Menninger)

INTERNET People who believe in freedom of expression have spent several centuries fighting against censorship, in whatever form. We have to be certain the 'Net' does not become the site for technological book burning. (JR Saul)

INVENTION ☺ The guy who invented the first wheel was an idiot. The guy who invented the other three, HE was a genius. (Sid Caesar)

INVENTION Invention, it must be humbly admitted, does not consist in creating out of void but out of chaos. (Mary Shelley)

INVENTION Benjamin Franklin may have discovered electricity but it was the man who invented the meter who made the money. (Earl Wilson)

INVENTION High heels were invented by a woman who had been kissed on the forehead. (C Morley)

INVENTION I just invent, then wait till man comes around to needing what I have invented. (B Fuller)

INVESTMENT Be fearful when others are greedy, and greedy when others are fearful. (Benjamin Graham)

INVESTMENT Investing in a startup does not make you an entrepreneur any more than buying a grand piano makes you a concert pianist. (Jeffrey Fry)

INVESTMENT Investing should be more like watching paint dry or watching grass grow. If you want excitement, take $800 and go to Las Vegas. (Paul Samuelson)

INVESTMENT   One of the funny things about the stock market is that every time one person buys, another sells, and both think they are astute. (W Feather)

INVESTMENT   The Stock market is a device to transfer money from the impatient to the patient. (Warren Buffett)

INVESTMENT   The United States has developed a new weapon that destroys people but it leaves buildings standing. It is called the stock market. (Jay Leno)

INVESTMENT   Wall street is the only place that people ride to in a Rolls-Royce to get advice from those who take the subway. (Warren Buffett)

INVESTMENT   There are no good or bad stocks. The company is either good or bad. Stocks are just stocks. (Kenneth L Fisher)

JOB ☺   The best way to appreciate your job is to imagine yourself without one. (Oscar Wilde)

JOKE   A person reveals his character by nothing so clearly as the joke he resents. (Lichtenberg)

JOKE   If there is one thing I know, it is that God does love a good joke. (Hugh Elliott)

JOURNALISM   Its failings notwithstanding, there is much to be said in favour of journalism in that by giving us the opinion of the uneducated, it keeps us in touch with the ignorance of the community. (Oscar Wilde)

JOURNALISM   In journalism, there has always been a tension between getting it first and getting it right. (Ellen Goodman)

JOURNALISM ☺   We journalists make it a point to know very little about an extremely wide variety of topics; this is how we stay objective. (Dave Barry)

JOURNALISM   Journalism is iterature in a hurry. (M Arnold)

JOURNALIST ☺   If a person is not talented enough to be a novelist, not smart enough to be a lawyer, and his hands are too shaky to perform operations, he becomes a journalist. (Norman Mailer)

JOY   In the fancy spectacle of life, aspire to find a joy that does not need an audience. (Joyce Rachelle)

JUSTICE   Law and justice are not always the same. (Gloria Steinem)

JUSTICE   I have always believed that to have true justice we must have equal harassment under the law. (Paul Krassner)

KINDNESS   Carry out a random act of kindness, with no expectation of reward, safe in the knowledge that one day someone might do the same for you. (Princess Diana)

KINDNESS   You cannot do a kindness too soon, for you never know how soon it will be too late. (Ralph Waldo Emerson)

KINDNESS Be kind, for everyone you meet is fighting a hard battle. (Socrates)

KINDNESS It is rather embarrassing to have given one's entire life to pondering the human predicament and to find that in the end one has little more to say than 'Try to be a little kinder'. (A Huxley)

KINDNESS   Those who bring sunshine to the lives of others cannot keep it from themselves. (JM Barrie)

KINDNESS A single act of kindness throws out roots in all directions, and the roots spring up and make new trees. (Amelia Earhart)

KINDNESS Be kind, for everyone you meet is fighting a hard battle. (Ian Maclaren)

KINDNESS I expect to pass through life but once. If therefore, there be any kindness I can show, or any good thing I can do to any fellow being, let me do it now, and not defer or neglect it, as I shall not pass this way again. (William Penn)

KINDNESS Kindness in words creates confidence. Kindness in thinking creates profoundness. Kindness in giving creates love. (Lao-tzu)

KINDNESS Kindness is a language the blind can see and the deaf can hear. (Mark Twain)

KINDNESS Kindness is the language that the deaf can hear and the blind can see. (Mark Twain)

KINDNESS There is no use doing a kindness if you do it a day too late. (Charles Kingsley)

KINDNESS Unexpected kindness is the most powerful, least costly, and most underrated agent of human change. (Bob Kerrey)

KINDNESS We can't heal the world today, but we can begin with a voice of compassion, a heart of love, and act of kindness. (Mary Davis)

KINDNESS Wise sayings often fall on barren ground, but a kind word is never thrown away. (Arthus Helps)

KINDNESS You have not lived a perfect day, even though you have earned your money, unless you have done something for someone who will never be able to repay you. (Ruth Smeltzer)

KISS   A kiss is a lovely trick designed by nature to stop speech when words become superfluous. (Ingrid Bergman)

KISS   The mouth is made for communication, and nothing is more articulate than a kiss. (Jarod Kintz)

KNOWLEDGE   I prefer tongue-tied knowledge to ignorant loquacity. (Cicero)

KNOWLEDGE   Where is the wisdom we have lost in knowledge? Where is the knowledge we have lost in information? (TS Eliot)

KNOWLEDGE   Knowledge which is acquired under compulsion obtains no hold on the mind. (Plato)

KNOWLEDGE   An investment in knowledge always pays the best interest. (Benjamin Franklin)

KNOWLEDGE   If a little knowledge is dangerous, where is the man who has so much as to be out of danger? (TH Huxley)

KNOWLEDGE   Knowledge has to be improved, challenged and increased constantly or it vanishes. (Peter Drucker)

KNOWLEDGE   Knowledge is not knowledge until someone else knows that one knows. (Lucilius)

KNOWLEDGE   Knowledge is of no value unless you put it into practice. (Anton Chekhov)

KNOWLEDGE   To know that we know what we know, and that we do not know what we do not know, that is true knowledge. (HD Thoreau)

KNOWLEDGE   Everyone you will ever meet knows something you don't. (Bill Nye)

KNOWLEDGE   If you understand everything, you must be misinformed. (Japanese proverb)

KNOWLEDGE   Never try to tell everything you know. It may take too short a time. (Norman Ford)

LABOUR   If everybody contemplates the infinite instead of fixing the drains, many of us will die of cholera. (John Rich)

LABOUR   Some are bent with toil, and some get crooked trying to avoid it. (HV Prochnow)

LADY ☺   Being powerful is like being a lady. If you have to tell people you are, you are not. (M Thatcher)

LANGUAGE   Be careful what you say. Words do not only describe reality. Words create reality. (Desmond Tutu)

LANGUAGE   A multitude of words is no proof of a prudent mind. (Thales)

LANGUAGE   Civilization began the first time an angry person cast a word instead of a rock. (Sigmund Freud)

LANGUAGE   Words unguarded cause distress. A single word has the power to destroy all other good that you may have done. Let not our words create doom, let them create positivity and hope. A single word, a moment's act, can slay love. (Sri Aurbindo)

LANGUAGE ☺   I once had a rose named after me, and I was very flattered. But I was not pleased to read the description in the catalog : no good in a bed, but fine up against a wall. (Eleanor Roosevelt)

LANGUAGE ☺   In Paris they simply stared when I spoke to them in French; I never did succeed in making those idiots understand their own language. (Mark Twain)

LANGUAGE   Boy, those French : they have a different word for everything. (Steve Martin)

LANGUAGE   Great literature is simply language charged with meaning to the utmost possible degree. (Ezra Pound)

LANGUAGE   Slang is a language that rolls up its sleeves, spits on its hands and goes to work. (Carl Sandburg)

LANGUAGE   There is a great power in words. If you don't hitch too many of them together. (Josh Billings)

LANGUAGE   Uttering a word is like striking a note on the keyboard of the imagination. (Ludwig Wittgenstein)

LAUGHTER   A day without laughter is a day wasted. (N Chamfort)

LAUGHTER   Laughter is an instant vacation. (Milton Berle)

LAUGHTER   Laughter is sunshine, it chases winter from the human face. (Victor Hugo)

LAUGHTER   If we couldn't laugh, we would all go insane. (Jimmy Buffett)

LAW   A lawsuit is a fruit tree planted in a lawyer's garden. (Italian proverb)

LAW   Anybody who thinks talk is cheap should get some legal advice. (FP Jones)

LAW   Law and order exist for the purpose of establishing justice and when they fail in this purpose they become the dangerously structured dams that block the flow of social progress. (ML King)

LAW   Never forget that everything Hitler did in Germany was legal. (ML King)

LAW   The law is reason free from passion. (Aristotle)

LAW   We are in bondage to the law so that we might be free. (Cicero)

LAW   No poet ever interpreted nature as freely as a lawyer interprets truth. (Jean Giraudoux)

LAW   I don't want a lawyer to tell me what I cannot do ; I hire him to tell me how to do what I want to do. (JP Morgan)

LAW   Laws are spider webs through which the big flies pass and the little ones get caught. (HD Balzac)

LAW   Nobody has a more sacred obligation to obey the law than those who make the law. (Sophocles)

LAW   The minute you read something you can't understand, you can almost be sure it was drawn up by a lawyer. (Will Rogers)

LAW   To quote me the authority of precedents leaves me quite unmoved. All human progress has been made by ignoring precedents. If mankind had continued to be slave of precedent we should still be living in caves and subsisting on shellfish and wild berries. (VP Snowden)

LAWS   Good people don't need laws to tell them to act responsibly..and bad people will find a way around the laws. (Plato)

LAZINESS When I hear about people making vast fortunes without doing any productive work or contributing anything to society, my reaction is, How do I get in on that? (Dave Barry)

LAZY ☺   I choose a lazy person to do a hard job. Because a lazy person will find an easy way to do it. (Bill Gates)

LEADER   If you would not follow yourself, why should anyone else? (JC Maxwell)

LEADER   Leadership is not about titles, positions or flowcharts. It is about one life influencing other. (JC Maxwell)

LEADER   Managers work with processes-leaders work with people. (JC Maxwell)

LEADER   When the leader lacks confidence, the followers lack commitment. (JC Maxwell)

LEADER   I must follow the people. Am I not their leader? (B Disraeli)

LEADER   It is hard to look up to a leader who keeps his ear to the ground. (JH Boren)

LEADER   The leader must know, must know that he knows, and must be able to make it abundantly clear to those around him that he knows. (Clarence B Randall)

LEADER   There go my people I must find out where they are going so I can lead them. (AL Rollin)

LEADERSHIP   You build your brand as a leader, not by making great speeches to thousands of people, but in conversation after conversation, one by one by one, making a small difference each time. (Tom Peters)

LEADERSHIP   No man will make a great leader who wants to do it all himself or get all the credit for doing it. (Andrew Carnegie)

LEADERSHIP   'May the force be with you' is charming, but it is not important. What is important is that you become the Force- for yourself and perhaps for other people. (Harrison Ford)

LEADERSHIP   A genuine leader is not a searcher for consensus but a moulder of consensus. (ML King Jr.)

LEADERSHIP   A good leader takes a little more than his share of the blame, a little less than his share of the credit. (AH Glasow)

LEADERSHIP   A leaders is one who knows the way, goes the way, and shows the way. (John C. Maxwell)

LEADERSHIP   A man who wants to lead the orchestra must turn his back on the crowd. (Max Lucado)

LEADERSHIP   Leadership is a privilege to better the life of others. It is not an opportunity to satisfy personal greed. (Mwai Kibaki)

LEADERSHIP   Leadership is not about the next election, it is about the next generation. (Simon Sinek)

LEADERSHIP   Leadership is practiced not so much in words as in attitude and in actions. (Harold S Geneen)

LEADERSHIP   Leadership, like swimming, cannot be learned by reading about it. (Henry Mintzberg)

LEADERSHIP   Management is doing things right, leadership is doing the right things. (Peter Drucker)

LEADERSHIP   People ask the difference between a leader and a boss. The leader leads, and the boss drives. (Theodore Roosevelt)

LEADERSHIP   People buy into the leader before they buy into the vision. (John C Maxwell)

LEADERSHIP   When the best leader's work is done, the people say, 'We did it ourselves'. (Lao Tzu)

LEADERSHIP   The great leaders have always stage-managed their effects. (Charles de Gaulle)

LEADERSHIP   The real leader has no need to lead, he is content to point the way. (Henry Miller)

LEADERSHIP   There has not been a great leader in this century who was not devious at certain times when it was necessary to achieve his goals. (Clinton Rossiter)

LEARNING   God may be in the details, but the goddess is in the questions. Once we begin to ask them, there is no turning back. (Gloria Steinem)

LEARNING   Once you have learned to ask questions- relevant and appropriate and substantial questions- you have learned how to learn and no one can keep you from learning whatever you want or need to know. (Neil Postman)

LEARNING   The years teach much, which the days never know. (RW Emerson)

LEARNING Formal education will make you a living, self-education will make you a fortune. (Jim Rohn)

LEARNING I am always ready to learn but I do not always like being taught. (Winston Churchill)

LEARNING In Japan we have the phrase shoshin, which means 'beginner's mind'. This does not mean a closed mind, but actually an empty mind and a ready mind. If your mind is empty, it is always ready for anything. It is open to everything. In the beginner's mind there are many possibilities, in the expert's mind there are few. (Shunryu Suzuki)

LEARNING In times of change, the learner will inherit the earth while the learned are beautifully equipped for a world that no longer exists. (Eric Hoffer)

LEARNING It is impossible to begin to learn that which one thinks one already knows. (Epictetus)

LEARNING Life is really simple, but we insist on making it complicated...By three methods we may learn wisdom : First, by reflection, which is noblest ; second, by imitation, which is easiest ; and third, by experience, which is the bitterest. (Confucius)

LEARNING Never learn to do anything ; if you don't learn, you will always find someone else to do it for you. (Mark Twain)

LEARNING That is what learning is : You suddenly understand something you have understood all your life, but in a new way. (Doris Lessing)

LEARNING The illiterate of the 21st century will not be those who cannot read and write, but those who cannot learn, unlearn and relearn. (Alvin Toffler)

LEARNING Try to learn something about everything, and everything about something. (TH Huxley)

LEGACY A good character is the best tombstone. Those who loved you and were helped by you will remember you when forget-me-nots have withered. Carve your name on hearts, not on marble. (Charles Spurgeon)

LEGACY If you would not be forgotten as soon as you are dead, either write things worth reading or do things worth writing. (Benjamin Franklin)

LEISURE Only a person who can live with himself can enjoy the gift of leisure. (Henry Greber)

LIBERAL No man can call himself liberal, or radical, or even a conservative advocate of fair play, if his work depends in any way on the unpaid or underpaid labor of women at home, or in the office. (Gloria Steinem)

LIBERTY Disobedience is the true foundation of liberty. The obedient must be slaves. (Thoreau)

LIBERTY Liberty means responsibility. That is why most men dread it. (GB Shaw)

LIBERTY People have only as much liberty as they have the intelligence to want and the courage to take. (Emma Goldman)

LIBERTY The only way to deal with an unfree world is to become so absolutely free that your very existence is an act of rebellion. (Albert Camus)

LIBERTY   Those who can give up essential liberty to obtain a little temporary safety deserve neither liberty nor safety. (Benjamin Franklin)

LIBRARY   A library is thought in cold storage. (Herbert Samuel)

LIE   People never lie so much as before an election, during a war, or after a hunt. (Otto von Bismarck)

LIE   The longer the explanation, the bigger the lie. (Chinese proverb)

LIE   He who permits himself to tell a lie once finds it much easier to do it a second and a third time till at length it becomes habitual. (Thomas Jefferson)

LIE   The liar's punishment is not in the least that he is not believed but that he cannot believe anyone else. (GB Shaw)

LIE I lie to myself all the time. But I never believe me. (SE Hinton)

LIE The cruellest lies are often told in silence. (RL Stevenson)

LIFE   Anybody who has survived his childhood has enough information about life to last him the rest of his days. (Flannery O'Connor)

LIFE   Experience life in all possible ways good-bad, bitter-sweet, dark-light, summer-winter. Experience all the dualities. Don't be afraid of experience, because the more experience you have, the more mature you become. (Osho)

LIFE   In necessary things, unity; in disputed things, liberty; in all things, charity. (Richard Baxter)

LIFE   Learn to light a candle in the darkest moments of someone's life. Be the light that helps others see; it is what gives life its deepest significance. (Roy T. Bennett)

LIFE   Life is a big canvas, throw all the paint on it you can. (Danny Kaye)

LIFE   Life is a succession of lessons which must be lived to be understood. (Hellen Keller)

LIFE   Live in the sunshine, swim the sea, drink the wild air. (Ralph Waldo Emerson)

LIFE   The game of life is a game of boomerangs. Our thoughts, deeds and words return to us sooner or later with astounding accuracy. (RL Evan)

LIFE   We forge the chains we wear in life. (Charles Dickens)

LIFE   You can't connect the dots looking forward; you can only connect them looking backwards. So you have to trust that the dots will somehow connect in the future. You have to trust in something- your gut, destiny, life, karma, whatever. This approach has never let me down, and it has made all the difference in my life. (Steve Jobs)

LIFE   You don't get to choose how you are going to die. Or when. But you can decide how you are going to live now. (Joan Baez)

LIFE   Adapt what is useful, reject what is useless, and add what is specifically your own. (Bruce Lee)

LIFE   An individual human existence should be like a river — small at first, narrowly contained within its banks, and rushing passionately past rocks and over waterfalls. Gradually the river grows wider, the banks recede, the waters flow more quietly, and in the end, without any visible break, they become merged in the sea, and painlessly lose their individual being. (Bertrand Russell)

LIFE   Do not pray for an easy life, pray for the strength to endure a difficult one. (Bruce Lee)

LIFE   Don't brood. Get on with living and loving. You don't have forever. (EE Rexford)

LIFE   Good friends, good books, and a sleepy conscience: this is the ideal life. (Mark Twain)

LIFE   I don't believe in happy endings, but I do believe in happy travels, because ultimately, you die at a very young age, or you live long enough to watch your friends die. It is a mean thing, life. (George Clooney)

LIFE   I have learned that to be with those I like is enough. (Walt Whitman)

LIFE   I suggest taking the high road and have a little sense of humour and let things roll off your back. (Sally Ride)

LIFE   In between goals is a thing called life, that has to be lived and enjoyed. (Joubert Botha)

LIFE   It is a very funny thing about life; if you refuse to accept anything but the best, you very often get it. (WS Maugham)

LIFE   Life is a series of natural and spontaneous changes. Don't resist them; that only creates sorrow. Let reality be a reality. Let things flow naturally forward in whatever way they like. (Lao Tzu)

LIFE   Life is like a ten speed bike. Most of us have gears we never use. (Charles Schultz)

LIFE   Life is like topography, Hobbes. There are summits of happiness and success, flat stretches of boring routine, and valleys of frustration and failure. (Calvin & Hobbes)

LIFE   Life is mostly froth and bubble. Two things stand like stone, kindness in another's trouble, courage in your own. (AL Gordon)

LIFE   Life is not about waiting for the storm to pass but learning to dance in the rain. (Vivian Greene)

LIFE   Life is not lost by dying ; life is lost minute by minute, day by dragging day, in all the thousand small uncaring ways. (SV Benet)

LIFE   Life is thickly sown with thorns, and I know no other remedy than to pass quickly through them. The longer we dwell on our misfortunes, the greater is their power to harm us. (Voltaire)

LIFE   Life isn't about getting and having, it's about giving and being. (Kevin Kruse)

LIFE   Live not like a flower, you will disintegrate the day you blossom, live like a stone, for once when carved, you will be a form of god. (HR Bachchan)

LIFE   Many people want to change their life but they are not willing to change their choices. (MJ De Marco)

LIFE   Some days there won't be a song in your heart. Sing anyway. (Emory Austin)

LIFE   The good life, as I conceive it, is a happy life. I do not mean that if you are good you will be happy; I mean that if you are happy you will be good. (Bertrand Russell)

LIFE   The same stream of life that runs through my veins night and day runs through the world and dances in rhythmic measures.(RN Tagore)

LIFE   The soul is born old but grows young. That is the comedy of life. And the body is born young and grows old. That is life's tragedy. (Oscar Wilde)

LIFE   The truth is, everyone is going to hurt you. You just got to find the ones worth suffering for. (Bob Marley)

LIFE   Those who don't feel this love pulling them like a river, those who don't drink dawn like a cup of spring water or take in sunset like a supper, those who don't want to change, let them sleep. (Rumi)

LIFE   When I look back on all these worries, I remember the story of the old man who said on his deathbed that he had had a lot of trouble in his life, most of which had never happened. (Winston Churchill)

LIFE ☺   We all pay for life with death, so everything in between should be free. (Bill Hicks)

LIFE ☺   For The happiest life, days should be rigorously planned, nights left open to chance. (M McLaughlin)

LIFE ☺   I believe you should live each day as if it is your last, which is why I don't have any clean laundry, because, come on, who wants to wash cloths on the last day of their life? (Albert Einstein)

LIFE ☺   What is human life? The first third a good time ; the rest remembering about it. (Mark Twain)

LIFE   A man sooner or later discovers that he is the master-gardener of his soul, the director of his life. (James Allen)

LIFE   As I grow to understand life less and less, I learn to live it more and more. (Jules Renard)

LIFE   As long as you keep a person down, some part of you has to be down, there to hold him down, so it means you cannot soar as you otherwise might. (Marian Anderson)

LIFE   Be faithful in small things because it is in them that your strength lies. (Mother Teresa)

LIFE   Celebrate what you want to see more of. (Tom Peters)

LIFE   Do not lose hold of your dreams or aspirations. For if you do, you may still exist but you have ceased to live. (Thoreau)

LIFE   Don't compare yourself with anyone in this world, if you do so, you are insulting yourself. (Bill Gates)

LIFE   Don't ever slam a door, you might want to go back. (Don Herold)

LIFE   Doubt is an uncomfortable condition, but certainty is a ridiculous one. (Voltaire)

LIFE   Dwell on the beauty of life. Watch the stars, and see yourself running with them. (Marcus Aurelius)

LIFE   Eating words has never given me indigestion. (Winston Churchill)

LIFE   Finish each day before you begin the next, and interpose a solid wall of sleep between the two.(Ralph Waldo Emerson)

LIFE   First secure an independent income, then practice virtue. (Greek proverb)

LIFE   Growth and comfort do not co-exist. (Ginni Rometty)

LIFE   He who has a why to live can bear almost any how. (F Nietzsche)

LIFE   I always did something I was a little not ready to do. I think that is how you grow. When there is that moment of 'Wow, I am not really sure I can do this', and you push through those moments, that is when you have a breakthrough. (Marissa Mayer)

LIFE   I challenge anybody in their darkest moment to write what they are grateful for, even stupid little things like green grass or a friendly conversation with somebody on the elevator. You start to realize how rich you are. (Jim Carrey)

LIFE   I have found some of the best reasons I ever had for remaining at the bottom simply by looking at the men at the top. (FM Colby)

LIFE   I will pay more for the ability to deal with people than any other ability under the sun. (JD Rockefeller)

LIFE   I will permit no one to narrow and degrade my soul by making me hate them. (Booker T. Washington)

LIFE   I've been popular and unpopular, successful and unsuccessful, loved and loathed. and I know how meaningless it all is. Therefore I feel free to take whatever risks I want. (Madonna)

LIFE   If I had my life to live over again, I would have made a rule to read some poetry and listen to some music at least once every week. (Charles Darwin)

LIFE   If more of us valued food and cheer and song above hoarded gold, it would be a merrier world. (J.R.R. Tolkien)

LIFE   If your heart is a volcano, how shall you expect flowers to bloom? (K Gibran)

LIFE   Imagination provides the wings for life's airplanes ; work, the motor. (BC Forbes)

LIFE   In order to go on living one must try to escape the death involved in perfectionism. (Hannah Arendt)

LIFE   In pursuit of your passions, always be young. In your relationships with others, always be a grown-up. (Tom Brokaw)

LIFE   In three words I can sum up everything I've learned about life: it goes on. (Robert Frost)

LIFE   It is not true that life is one damn thing after another- it's one damn thing over and over. (Edna Millay)

LIFE   It is your road and yours alone, others may walk it with you, but no one can walk it for you. (Rumi)

LIFE   Keep me away from the wisdom which does not cry, the philosophy which does not laugh and the greatness which does not bow before children. (Khalil Gibran)

LIFE   Keep your broken arm inside your sleeve. (Chinese proverb)

LIFE   Lessons in life will be repeated until they are learned. (Frank Sonnenberg)

LIFE   Let there be spaces in your togetherness. (K Gibran)

LIFE   Let us endeavour so to live that when we come to die even the undertaker will be sorry. (Mark Twain)

LIFE   Letting go does not always equate to you losing or missing out. You are growing, you are shedding, you are becoming. (Alex Elle)

LIFE   Life can only be understood backwards ; but it must be lived forwards. (Soren Kierkegaard)

LIFE   Life has a way of forcing decisions on those who vacillate. (Nelson Mandela)

LIFE   Life is a dream for the wise, a game for the fool, a comedy for the rich, a tragedy for the poor. (Sholom Aleichem)

LIFE   Life is a shipwreck, but we must not forget to sing in the lifeboats. (Voltaire)

LIFE   Life is a train of moods like a string of beads, and as we pass through them, they prove to be many-coloured lenses which paint the world their own hue, and each shows only what lies in its focus. (RW Emerson)

LIFE   Life is about moments ; Don't wait for them, create them. (Tony Robbins)

LIFE   Life is easier to take than you would think ; all that is necessary is to accept the impossible, do without the indispensable and bear the intolerable. (K Norris)

LIFE   Life is like a 10-speed bike. Most of us have gears we never use. (Charles M Schulz)

LIFE   Life is like a blanket too short. You pull it up and your toes rebel, you yank it down and shivers meander about your shoulder ; but cheerful folks manage to draw their knees up and pass a very comfortable night. (Marion Howard)

LIFE   Life is like playing a violin in public and learning the instrument as one goes on. (S Butler)

LIFE   Life is like riding a taxi ; whether you are going anywhere or not , the meter keeps ticking. (John Maxwell)

LIFE   Life is not a problem to be solved, but a reality to be experienced. (Kierkegaard)

LIFE   Life is not about finding yourself. Life is about creating yourself. (GB Shaw)

LIFE   Life is what happens to you while you are busy making other plans. (John Lennon)

LIFE   Life will bring you pain all by itself. Your responsibility is to create joy. (Milton Erickson)

LIFE   Life would be infinitely happier if we could only be born at the age of eighty and gradually approach eighteen. (Mark Twain)

LIFE   Like Alexander the Great and Casar, Ito conquer the world. But first I have to top at Walmart and pick up some supplies. (J Kintz)

LIFE   Live in the remembrance of your true nature - the eternal, infinite and unchanging Self. You will experience fearlessness, peace and joy. (Swami Avdheshanand)

LIFE   Make it your mission to magnify people's strengths, not to highlight their weaknesses. (Lorri Faye)

LIFE   Man, unlike the animals, has never learned that the sole purpose of life is to enjoy it. (Samuel Butler)

LIFE   May you live all the days of your life. (J Swift)

LIFE   Millions long for immortality who do not know what to do with themselves on a rainy Sunday afternoon. (Susan Ertz)

LIFE   My grandfather always said that living is like licking honey off a thorn. (L Adamic)

LIFE   Never look back unless you are planning to go that way. (HD Thoreau)

LIFE   None of us are getting out of here alive, so please stop treating yourself like an afterthought. Eat the delicious food. Walk in the sunshine. Jump in the ocean. Say the truth that you are carrying in your heart like hidden treasure. Be silly, Be kind. Be weird. There is no time for anything else. (Anthony Hopkins)

LIFE   Often when you think you are at the end of something, you are at the beginning of something else. (Fred Rogers)

LIFE   One learns in life to keep silent and draw one's own confusions. (CO Skinner)

LIFE   Realize deeply that the present moment is all you ever have. (Eckhart Tolle)

LIFE   Renown is a source of toil and sorrow ; obscurity is a source of happiness. (J Mosheim)

LIFE   Showing up is 80 percent of life. (Woody Allen)

LIFE   Some people feel the rain. Others just get wet. (Bob Marley)

LIFE   Take care to sell your horse before he dies. The art of life is passing losses on. (Robert Frost)

LIFE   The best investment you can make is in yourself. (Warren Buffett)

LIFE   The cost of a thing is the amount of what I call life which is required to be exchanged for it, immediately or in the long run. (HD Thoreau)

LIFE   The dignity of man lies in his ability to face reality in all its meaninglessness. (M Esslin)

LIFE   The hardest thing to learn in life is which bridge to cross and which to burn. (David Russell)

LIFE   The inspiration you seek is already within you. Be silent and listen. (Rumi)

LIFE   The key to immortality is first living a life worth remembering. (Bruce Lee)

LIFE   The lion cannot protect himself from traps, and the fox cannot defend himself from wolves. One must therefore be a fox to recognize traps, and a lion to frighten wolves. (Machiavelli)

LIFE   The master in the art of living makes little distinction between his work and his play, his labor and his leisure, his mind and his body, his information and his recreation, his love and his religion. He hardly knows which is which. He simply pursues his vision of excellence at whatever he does, leaving others to decide whether he is working or playing. To him he's always doing both. (James A. Michener)

LIFE   The one serious conviction that a man should have is that nothing is to be taken too seriously. (S Butler)

LIFE   The second half of a man's life is made up of nothing but the habits he has acquired during the first half. (F Dostoevski)

LIFE   The secret of health for both mind and body is not to mourn for the past, nor to worry about the future, but to live the present moment wisely and earnestly. (Buddha)

LIFE   The secret of life is honesty and fair dealing. If you can fake that, you have got it made. (Groucho Marx)

LIFE   The secret to a rich life is to have more beginnings than endings. (Dave Weinbaum)

LIFE   The secret to living well and longer is : eat half, walk double, laugh triple and love without measure. (Tibetan proverb)

LIFE   The walls we build around us to keep sadness out also keep out the joy. (Jim Rohn)

LIFE   The world is a comedy to those that think, a tragedy to those that feel. (Horace Walpole)

LIFE   There are two educations. One should teach us how to make a living and the other how to live. (John Adams)

LIFE   There is no moral percept that does not have something inconvenient about it. (Denis Diderot)

LIFE   There is no one way to dance. And that is kind of my philosophy about everything. (Ellen Degeneres)

LIFE   There is only one thing about which I am certain, and that is that there is very little about which one can be certain. (W Somerset Maugham)

LIFE   To live is the rarest thing in the world. Most people exist, that is all. (Oscar Wilde)

LIFE   Too many of us are not living our dreams because we are living our fears. (Les Brown)

LIFE   We all die. The goal is not to live forever, the goal is to create something that will. (Chuck Palahniuk)

LIFE   We are never prepared for what we expect. (James A Michener)

LIFE   We never really grow up, we only learn how to act in public. (Bryan White)

LIFE   Were it offered to my choice, I should have no objections to a repetition of the same life from its beginning, only asking the advantages authors have in a second edition to correct some faults of the first. (B Franklin)

LIFE   What is the point of being alive if you don't at least try to do something remarkable? (John Green)

LIFE   Whatever we treasure for ourselves separates us from others; our possessions are our limitations. (R Tagore)

LIFE   When one has great gifts, what answer to the meaning of existence should one require beyond the right to exercise them? (WH Auden)

LIFE   Wound is the place where life enters you. (Rumi)

LIFE   You are not a drop in the ocean. You are the entire ocean in a drop. (Rumi)

LIFE   You are only given a little spark of madness. You must not lose it. (Robin Williams)

LIFE   You can have it all. Just not all at once. (Oprah Winfrey)

LIFE   You got to go down a lot of wrong roads to find the right one. (Bob Parsons)

LIFE   You have got to get to the stage in life where going for it is more important than winning or losing. (Arthur Ashe)

LIFE   You were born with wings. Why prefer to crawl through life? (Rumi)

LIKE   I dont like her. But dont misunderstand me : my dislike is purely platonic. (Sir HB Tree)

LISTENING   Few human beings are proof against the implied flattery of rapt attention. (Jack Woodford)

LOAN   Someone has suggested that America's greatest gifts to civilization are three : cornflakes, Kleenex and credit. (Louis T. Benezet)

LOSS   You just need to be nice to yourself sometimes after a loss. (Venus Williams)

LOSS   If you don't fight for what you want, don't cry for what you lost. (Will Smith)

LOSS   Win without boasting. Lose without excuse. (AP Terhune)

LOVE   One word frees us of all the weight and pain of life: That word is love. (Sophocles)

LOVE   The way to love anything is to realize that it might be lost.   (Robert Cialdini)

LOVE   I think the biggest disease the world suffers from in this day and age is the disease of people feeling unloved. I know that I can give love for a minute, for half an hour, for a day, for a month, but I can give. I am very happy to do that, I want to do that. (Princess Diana)

LOVE   Love is a fire. But whether it is going to warm your hearth or burn down your house, you can never tell. (Joan Crawford)

LOVE   Love is a gift of one's inner most soul to another so both can be whole. (Buddha)

LOVE   The greatest love is a mother's; then a dog's; then a sweetheart's. (Polish proverb)

LOVE   You can never know anyone as completely as you want. But that is okay, love is better. (Caroline Paul)

LOVE   You may be hurt if you love too much, but you will live in misery if you love too little. (Napoleon Hill)

LOVE   Loving, like driving, is best done when you don't think about the gear changes. (S Bandopadhyay)

LOVE ☺   A pair of powerful spectacles has sometimes sufficed to cure a person in love. (F Nietzsche)

LOVE ☺   All you need is love. But a little chocolate now and then does not hurt. (C Schultz)

LOVE ☺   Loving, like driving, is best done when you don't think about the gear changes. (S Bandopadhyay)

LOVE   To love or have loved, that is enough. Ask nothing further. There is no other pearl to be found in the dark folds of life. (Victor Hugo)

LOVE   I love neither with my heart nor with my mind. Just in case the heart might stop, the mind can forget. I love with my soul. The soul never stops or forgets. (Rumi)

LOVE   I love you not because of who you are, but because of who I am when I am with you. (Roy Croft)

LOVE   I love you, and because I love you, I would sooner have you hate me for telling you the truth than adore me for telling you lies. (Pietro Aretino)

LOVE   It is not love that should be depicted as blind, but self-love. (Voltaire)

LOVE   Love a person the way they need to be loved, not the way you want to love. It is not about you. Love is selfless, not selfish. (Tony Gaskins)

LOVE   Love does not just sit there, like a stone, it has to be made, like bread, remade all the time, made new. (Ursula K.Le Guin)

LOVE   Love is an irresistible desire to be irresistibly desired. (Robert Frost)

LOVE   Love is everything it's cracked up to be. That's why people are so cynical about it. It really is worth fighting for, being brave for, risking everything for. And the trouble is, if you don't risk anything, you risk even more. (Erica Jung)

LOVE   Love is like a seaweed ; even if you have pushed it away, you will not prevent it from coming back. (Nigerian proverb)

LOVE   Love is of all passions the strongest, for it attacks simultaneously the head, the heart and the senses.. (Lao Tzu)

LOVE   Love is saying 'I feel differently' instead of 'You are wrong'. (Brandi Synder)

LOVE   Love is the condition in which the happiness of another person is essential to your own. (Robert Heinlein)

LOVE   Love is the net where hearts are caught like fish. (Muhammad Ali)

LOVE   Love is the only thing in this world that is unequivocal. There are different kinds of love, certainly, but it is a you-do or you-don't proposition with them all. (Harper Lee)

LOVE   Love is the water of life. Nurturing heart and soul. (Rumi)

LOVE   Love is the word used to label the sexual excitement of the young, the habituation of the middle-aged, and the mutual dependence of the old. (John Ciardi)

LOVE   Love isn't finding a perfect person. It's seeing an imperfect person perfectly. (Sam Keen)

LOVE   Never love anyone who treats you like you are ordinary. (Oscar Wilde)

LOVE   Platonic love is love form the neck up. (TS Winslow)

LOVE   To love is to admire with the heart ; to admire is to love with the mind. (T Gautier)

LOVE   You know it's love when all you want is that person to be happy, even if you are not part of their happiness. (Julia Roberts)

LOYALTY   You can buy people's time, you can buy their physical presence at a given place, you can even buy a measured number of their skilled muscular motions per hour. But you cannot buy enthusiasm, you cannot buy loyalty, you cannot buy the devotion of hearts, minds or souls. You must earn these. (Clarence Francis)

LUCK   Fortune knocks but once, but misfortune has much more patience. (LJ Peter)

LUCK   You never know what worse luck your bad luck has saved you from. (Cormac McCarthy)

LUCK   Everything comes to the man who does not need it. (French proverb)

LUCK   Luck is what happens when preparation meets opportunity. (Seneca)

LUCK   People always call it luck when you have acted more sensibly than they have. (Anne Tyler)

LUXURY   Luxury goods are the only area in which it is possible to make luxury margins. (Bernard Arnault)

LUXURY   One of history's few iron laws is that luxuries tend to become necessities and to spawn new obligations. (Yuval Noah Harari)

LUXURY   Luxury is the ease of a t-shirt in a very expensive dress. (karl Lagerfeld)

LUXURY   Real luxury is a balance between quality and the affection you feel for an object that cannot be easily replicated. (Marco Zanini)

LUXURY   Some people think that luxury is the opposite of poverty. It is not. It is the opposite of vulgarity. (Coco Chanel)

MACHINE One machine can do the work of fifty ordinary men. No machine can do the work of one extraordinary man. (E Hubbard)

MACHINE The real question is not whether machines think but whether men do. (BF Skinner)

MAN   Every man as his faults. It all depends on whether he has enough good qualities to counterbalance them. (F Santa)

MAN   The perfect man? A poet on a motorcycle. (Lucinda Williams)

MANAGEMENT   So much of what we call management consists in making it difficult for people to work. (Peter Drucker)

MANAGER No amount of policies and procedure, fancy cafeterias, generous fringe benefits, or sparkling toilets can take the place of the seniors (supervisors) who are interested in their people and treat them wisely & well. (J.Bittel)

MANNERISM   My father had taught me to be nice first, because you can always be mean later, but once you've been mean to someone, they won't believe the nice anymore. So be nice, be nice, until it's time to stop being nice, then destroy them. (Laurell Hamilton)

MANNERISM   You should not interrupt my interruptions. That is really worse than interrupting. (TS Eliot)

MANNERS Respect for ourselves guides our morals ; respect for others guides our manners. (Laurence)

MARKET Markets are constantly in a state of uncertainty and flux, and money is made by discounting the obvious and betting on the unexpected. (G Soros)

MARRAIGE   In every marriage more than a week old, there are grounds for divorce. The trick is to find and continue to find grounds for marriage. (R Anderson)

MARRAIGE Matromony is a process by which a grocer acquired an account the florist had. (Francis Rodman)

MARRAIGE		The critical period in matrimony is breakfast time. (AP Herbert)

MARRIAGE ☺		Marriage is the triumph of imagination over intelligence. Second marriage is the triumph of hope over experience. (Oscar Wilde)

MARRIAGE		After a few years of marriage a man can look right at a woman without seeing her and a woman can see right through a man without looking at him. (Helen Rowland)

MARRIAGE		I know enough to know that no woman should ever marry a man who hated his mother. (Martha Gellhorn)

MARRIAGE		If a marriage needs help, the answer almost always is have more fun. Drop your list of grievances and go ride a roller coaster. (Garrison Keillor)

MARRIAGE		Love at first sight is easy to understand. It is when two people have been looking at each other for years that it becomes a miracle. (Sam Levenson)

MARRIAGE		Love is the dawn of marriage, and marriage is the sunset of love. (French proverb)

MARRIAGE		Marriage is a great institution, but I am not ready for an institution, yet. (Mae West)

MARRIAGE		Marriage is for women the commonest mode of livelihood, and the total amount of undesired sex endured by women is probably greater in marriage than in prostitution. (B Russell)

MARRIAGE   Marriage is when a man and woman become as one ; the trouble starts when they try to decide which one. (Mae West)

MARRIAGE   Often the difference between a successful marriage and a mediocre one consists of leaving about three or four things a day unsaid. (H Miller)

MARRIAGE   The difficulty with marriage is that we fall in love with a personality, but must live with a character. (Peter De Vries)

MARRIAGE   You know it is never fifty-fifty in a marriage. It is always seventy-thirty, or sixty-forty. Someone falls in love first. Someone puts someone else up on a pedestal. Someone works very hard to keep things rolling smoothly ; someone else sails along for the ride. (Jodi Picoult)

MEANING When you draw or paint a tree, you do not imitate a tree; you do not copy it exactly as it is, which would be mere photography. To be free to paint a tree or flower or sunset, you have to feel what it conveys to you : the significance, the meaning of it. (J Krishnamurti)

MEDICINE One of the first duties of the physician is to educate the masses not to take medicine. (William Osler)

MEDICINE The art of medicine consists of amusing the patient while nature cures the disease. (Voltaire)

MEDICINE The pen is mightier than the sword ! The case for prescription rather than surgery. (Marvin Kitman)

MEDIOCRITY   Being realistic is the most commonly traveled road to mediocrity. (Will Smith)

MEDIOCRITY   Any sort of pretension induces mediocrity in art and life alike. (M Fonteyn)

MEMORIES   Like mulligatawny soup in a cheap restaurant, memories are best not stirred. (PG Wodehouse)

MEMORY Do not forget small kindnesses and do not remember small faults. (Chinese Proverb)

MEMORY Some of us think holding on makes us strong ; but sometimes it's letting go. (H Hesse)

MEMORY What matters in life is not what happens to you but what you remember and how you remember it. (Gabriel Garcia Marquez)

MEMORY   Every man's memory is his private literature. (A Huxley)

MEMORY   Memory is a crazy woman that hoards colored rags and throws away food. (Austin O'Malley)

MEMORY   Nothing fixes a thing so intensely in the memory as the wish to forget it. (Montaigne)

MEMORY   The advantage of a bad memory is that one enjoys several times the same good things for the first time. (Nietzsche)

MEMORY   There is nothing like an odour to stir memories. (W Mcfee)

MEN   A man takes real notice of a woman only after another man takes notice of her (F Molnar)

MEN   A weapon men use against women is the refusal to take them seriously. (David Mitchell)

MEN   It is absolutely unfair for women to say that guys only want one thing : sex. We also want food. (Jarod Kintz)

MEN   Women are not embarrassed when they buy men's pyjamas, but a man buying a nightgown acts as though he were dealing with a dope peddler. (Jimmy Cannon)

MENTOR   Anyone who ever gave you confidence, you owe them a lot.   (Truman Capote)

MENTOR   If you treat an individual as he is, he will remain as he is. But if you treat him as he were what he ought to be and could be, he will become what he ought to be and could be. (Goethe)

MENTOR   We must view young people not as empty bottles to be filled, but as candles to be lit. (Robert H.Shaffer)

MENTORING   When I give a man an office, I watch him carefully to see whether he is swelling or growing. (Woodrow Wilson)

MERCY   Mercy to the guilty is cruelty to the innocent. (Adam Smith)

MIND   Our greatest battles are with our own minds. (Jameson Frank)

MIND   Tension is who you think you should be, relaxation is who you are. (Chinese proverb)

MIND   To enjoy good health, to bring true happiness to one's family, to bring peace to all – one must first discipline and control one's own mind. If a man can control his mind he can find the way to enlightenment. (Gautam Buddha)

MIND   We deal with our mind from morning till evening, and it can be our best friend or our worst enemy. (M Ricard)

MIND   You have got to win in your mind before you win in your life. (John Addison)

MIND   The mind can changed the brain, and a changed brain can then change the mind. (Dr. Richard Davidson)

MIND   The trouble with most people is that they think with their hopes or fears or wishes rather than with their minds. (Nancy Astor)

MIND   Peace of mind is that mental condition in which you have accepted the worst. (Lin Yutang)

MIND   The snake which cannot cast its skin has to die. As well the minds which are prevented from changing their opinions, they cease to be mind. (F Nietzsche)

MIND   A positive mind looks for ways it can be done, a negative mind looks for ways it can't be done. (N Hill)

MIND   Great minds discuss ideas, average minds discuss events, small minds discuss people. (E. Roosevelt)

MIND   If your mind is not open, keep your mouth shut too. (Sue Grafton)

MIND   It is the mark of an educated mind to be able to entertain a thought without accepting it. (Aristotle)

MIND   It requires a very unusual mind to make an analysis of the obvious. (Alfred North Whitehead)

MIND   May this mind of mine, that immortal spirit, by which all past and present world is comprehended, by which all benevolent works are promoted and conducted resolve on what is nobel. (Yajurveda)

MIND   Mindfulness is a way of befriending ourselves and our experience. (Jon Kabat-Zinn)

MIND   Minds are like parachutes. They only function when they are open. (James Dewar)

MIND   The energy of the mind is the essence of life. (Aristotle)

MIND   The intuitive mind is a sacred gift and the rational mind is a faithful servant. We have created a society that honours the servant and has forgotten the gift. (Albert Einstein)

MIND   The mind once enlightened cannot again become dark. (Thomas Paine)

MIND   The professional mind is so microscopic that it sometimes ceases to be binocular. (Bernard De Voto)

MIND   The trouble with having an open mind, of course, is that people will insist on coming along and trying to put things in it. (Terry Pratchett)

MIND   There are three strengths of the mind : Will power (ichha shakti), Knowledge power (jnana shakti) and creative power (kriya shakti). (Swami N. Saraswati)

MIND   Your calm mind is the ultimate weapon against your challenges. So relax. (Bryant McGill)

MIND-CONTROL A person who remains focussed and balanced at all times is of steady mind. He is not elated unreasonably at times of happiness and is not disturbed by adversities and is free from attachment, fear and anger. (The Gita 2/56)

MIND-CONTROL He to whom joy is no joy and sorrow is no sorrow and whose heart is not agitated even while being engaged in pleasure- he who rejoices in pure consciousness itself, as well as in the objective world, is a liberated one. (Sage Vasishta in Yoga Vasishta)

MINDFULNESS   Mindfulness is about you. It is about overcoming the multi-tasking trap, and entering the attention economy, being one second ahead of your wandering mind and external distractions. It is about being the best version of yourself every day. (R Hougaard)

MINDFULNESS   Mindfulness is paying attention, on purpose, in the present moment, non-judgementally. (Jon Kabat-Zinn)

MINDSET If you want to love what you do, abandon the passion mindset ("what can the world offer me?") and instead adopt the craftsman mindset ("what can I offer the world?")." (Cal Newport)

MINING   Mining is like a search-and-destroy mission. Stewart Udall)

MINORITY The smallest minority on earth is the individual. Those who deny individual rights cannot claim to be defenders of minorities. (Ayn Rand)

MIRROR ☺ I was just viciously body-shamed by mirror. (Danny Zuker)

MISERY   Misery develops in the insidious seams created by imprecision and faulty human thinking. The cure for unhappiness is finding joy by embracing human nature. (Kilroy J. Oldster)

MISTAKE All men make mistakes, but a good man yields when he knows his course is wrong, and repairs the evil. The only crime is pride. (Sophocles)

MISTAKE Everyone makes mistakes ; no one is perfect : "A man should never be ashamed to own he has been in the wrong, which is but saying, in other words, that he is wiser today than he was yesterday." (Alexander Pope)

MISTAKE   Mistakes are always forgivable if one has the courage to admit them. (Bruce Lee)

MISTAKE   More people would learn from their mistakes if they weren't so busy denying them. (Harold J Smith)

MISTAKE   The greatest mistake you can make in life is to be continually fearing you will make one. (Elbert Hubbard)

MISTAKE   There is nothing to be learned from the second kick of a mule. (Mark Twain)

MISTAKE   A man should never be ashamed to own that he has been in the wrong, which is but saying in other words that he is wiser today than he was yesterday. (Alexander Pope)

MISTAKE   Even a mistake may turn out to be the one thing necessary to a worthwhile achievement. (Henry Ford)

MOB   The nose of a mob is its imagination. By this, at any time, it can be quietly led. (Edgar Allen Poe)

MOB   The nose of a mob is its imagination. By this, at any time, it can be quietly led. (Edgar Allan Poe)

MODERATION   It is possible to own too much. A man with one watch knows what time it is, a man with two watches is never quite sure. (Lee Segall)

MODESTY The English instinctively admire any man who has no talent and is modest about it. (James Agee)

MONEY   A man wants to earn money in order to be happy, and his whole effort and the best of a life are devoted to the earning of that money. Happiness is forgotten; the means are taken for the end. (Albert Camus)

MONEY   A rich man never fails to spot dropped coins. (Kautilya)

MONEY   Don't think money does everything or you are going to end up doing everything for money. (Voltaire)

MONEY   It is a kind of spiritual snobbery that makes people think they can be happy without money. (Albert Camus)

MONEY   A man who both spends and saves money is the happiest man, because he has both enjoyments. (Samuel Johnson)

MONEY   He has so much money that he could afford to look poor. (Edgar Wallace)

MONEY   He that is of the opinion money will do everything may well be suspected of doing everything for money. (Benjamin Franklin)

MONEY   I have got all the money I will ever need, just so long as I die by 4 o'clock. (H Youngman)

MONEY   I must say I hate money, but it is the lack of it I hate most. (Katherine Mansfield)

MONEY   I would like to live like a poor man only with lots of money. (Pablo Picasso)

MONEY   If you have no money, be polite. (Danish proverb)

MONEY   It is a kind of spiritual snobbery that makes people think they can be happy without money. (Albert Camus)

MONEY   It is amazing ; the moment you show cash, everyone knows your language. (Aravind Adiga)

MONEY   It is not enough for you to love money- it is also necessary that money should love you. (Baron Rothschild)

MONEY   It is not how much money you make, but how much money you keep, how hard it works for you, and how many generations you keep it for. (Robert Kiyosaki)

MONEY   It is said that for money you can have everything, but you cannot. You can buy food, but not appetite; medicine, but not health; knowledge, but not wisdom; glitter, but not beauty; fun, but not joy; acquaintances, but not friends; servants, but not faithfulness; leisure, but not peace. You can have the husk of everything for money, but not the kernel. (Arne Garborg)

MONEY   Money does not talk, it swears. (Bob Dylan)

MONEY   Money often costs too much. (RW Emerson)

MONEY   Money, if it does not bring you happiness, will at least help you be miserable in comfort. (HG Brown)

MONEY   Money-in its absence we are coarse, in its presence we are vulgar. (M McLaughlin)

MONEY   The chief value of money lies in the fact that one lives in a world in which it is overestimated. (HL Mencken)

MONEY   The only people who claim that money is not important are people who have enough money so that they are relieved of the ugly burden of thinking about it. (Joyce Carol Oates)

MONEY   The prosperous man is never sure that he is loved for himself. (Marcus Lucan)

MONEY   The rich man is always sold to the institution which makes him rich. Absolutely speaking, the more money, the less virtue. (HD Thoreau)

MONEY   There are more important things than money- the only thing is they all cost money. (LA Safian)

MONEY   Those who have some means think that the most important thing in the world is love. The poor know that it is money. (Gerald Brenon)

MONEY   To have money is to be virtuous, honest, beautiful and witty. And to be without it is to be ugly and boring and stupid and useless. (Jean Giradoux)

MONEY   When I was young I used to think that money was the most important thing in life, now that I am old, I know it is. (Oscar Wilde)

MONEY   When it is a question of money, everybody is of the same religion. (Voltaire)

MONEY   Whoever said money can't buy happiness simply didn't know where to go shopping. (Bo Derek)

MONEY   Money never goes to jail. (Arab proverb)

MONSTER Whoever fights monsters should see to it that in the process he does not become a monster. (Nietzsche)

MOOD It is easy to mistake the horrible for wonderful. You just have to be in the right mood. (PN Renu)

MOON The moon is always there, in our light and dark moments, changing forever just as we do. Every day it is a different version of itself- sometimes weak and wan ; sometimes strong and full of light. The moon understands what it means to be human : Uncertain. Alone. Cratered by imperfections. (T Mafi)

MORALITY Morality is its own advocate, it is never necessary to apologize for it. (Edith Harrell)

MOTHER A mother understands what a child does not say. (Jewish proverb)

MOTHER Autumn knows mother's heart. It gives and then lets go. (AW Crosby)

MOTHER Being a mother is learning about strengths you did not know you had, and dealing with fears you did not know existed. (Linda Wooten)

MOTHER If evolution really works, how come mothers only have two hands? (Milton Berle)

MOTHER Nowadays they say you need a special chip to put in the TV so kids can't watch this and that. In my day, we did not need a chip. My mum was the chip. End of story. (Ray Charles)

MOTHER They say our mothers really know how to push our buttons- because they installed them. (Robin Williams)

MOTIVATION   Always back the horse named self-interest, son. It will be the only one trying. (Jack Lang)

MOTIVE   It is useless to hold a person to anything he says when he is in love, drunk or running for office. (Shirley Maclaine)

MOTIVE   We would often be ashamed of our finest actions if the world understood all the motives which produced them. (Rochefoucauld)

MOVIE ☺   Never judge a book by its movie. (JW Eagan)

MUSIC   A painter paints pictures on canvas. But musicians paint their pictures on silence. (L Stokowski)

MUSIC   After silence, that which comes nearest to expressing the inexpressible is music. (Aldous Huxley)

MUSIC   If a composer could say what he had to say in words he would not bother trying to say it in music. (G Mahler)

MUSIC   Music gives a soul to the universe, wings to the mind, flight to the imagination and life to everything. (Plato)

MUSIC   Music is audible mathematics. (D Osmond)

MUSIC   Music is the mediator between the spiritual and the sensual life. (L Beethoven)

MUSIC   Music was my refuge. I could crawl into the space between the notes and curl my back to loneliness. (Maya Angelou)

MUSIC   Music washes away from the soul the dust of everyday life. (B Auerbach)

MUSIC   One good thing about music, when it hits you, you feel no pain. (Bob Marley)

MUSIC   Words make you think a thought. Music makes you feel a feeling. A song makes you feel a thought. (EY Harburg)

MUSIC   After silence, that which comes nearest to expressing the inexpressible is music. (A Huxley)

MUSIC   In music one must think with the heart and feel with the brain. (George Szell)

MUSIC   Music was my refuge. I could crawl into the space between the notes and curl my back to loneliness. (Maya Angelou)

MUSIC   No matter how corrupt, greedy, and heartless our government, our corporations, our media, and our religious & charitable institutions may become, the music will still be wonderful. (Kurt Vonnegut)

MUSIC   Singing is like a celebration of oxygen. (Bjork)

MUSIC   Music is a moral law. It gives soul to the universe, wings to the mind, flight to the imagination, and charm and gaiety to life and to everything. (Plato)

NATURE   Adopt the pace of nature: her secret is patience. (RW Emerson)

NATURE   Man is the most insane species. He worships an invisible God and destroys visible Nature. Unaware that this Nature he's destroying IS this God he's worshipping. (Hubert Reeves)

NATURE   Those who contemplate the beauty of the earth find reserves of strength that will endure as long as life lasts. There is something infinitely healing in the repeated refrains of nature — the assurance that dawn comes after night, and spring after winter. (Rachel Carson)

NATURE Thousands of tired, nerve-shaken, over-civilized people are beginning to find out that going to the mountains is going home; that wildness is a necessity. (John Muir)

NATURE   I don't understand why when we destroy something created by man we call it vandalism, but when we destroy something created by Nature we call it progress. (ED Begley Jr.)

NATURE   In every walk with nature, one receives far more than he seeks. (John Muir)

NATURE   Nature is proving that she can't be beaten- not by the likes of us. She's taking the world away from intellectuals and giving it back to the apes. (RE Sherwood)

NATURE   Poor indeed is the garden in which birds find no homes. (Abram L Urban)

NATURE   Thank God men cannot fly, and lay waste the sky as well as the earth. (HD Thoreau)

NEGOTIATION   We cannot negotiate with those who say, "What is mine is mine, what is yours is negotiable." (John F. Kennedy)

NEGOTIATION   The most difficult thing in any negotiation, almost, is making sure that you strip it of the emotion and deal with the facts. (Howard Baker)

NEWS   News is the first rough draft of history. (Ben Bradlee)

NEWS   News is what somebody somewhere wants to suppress. All the rest is advertising. (Lord Northcliffe)

NEWS   All the papers that matter live off their advertisements, and the advertisers exercise an indirect censorship over news. (George Orwell)

NEWSPAPER   A good newspaper, I suppose, is a nation talking to itself." (Arthur Miller)

NEWSPAPER   Trying to determine what is going on in the world by reading newspapers is like trying to tell the time by watching the second hand of a clock. (Ben Hecht)

NEWSPAPER ☺   It is amazing that the amount of news that happens in the world everyday always just exactly fits the newspaper. (Jerry Seinfeld)

NEWSPAPER   If you don't read the newspaper, you're uninformed. If you read the newspaper, you're mis-informed. (Mark Twain)

NEWSPAPER   One reason that cats are happier than people is that they have no newspapers. (Gwendolyn Brooks)

NOVELTY Every new beginning comes from some other beginning's end. (Seneca)

NOVELTY What the new year brings to you will depend a great deal on what you bring to the new year. (Vern Mclellan)

OBESITY   Obesity is a double victory for consumerism. Instead of eating little, which will lead to economic contraction, people eat too much and then buy diet products – contributing to economic growth twice over. (Yuval Noah Harari)

OBSESSION ☺ The best cure for an obsession ; get another one. (Mason Cooley)

OFFICE His insomnia was so bad, he could not sleep during office hours. (Arthur Baer)

OFFICE I always arrive late at the office, but I make up for it by leaving early. (Charles Lamb)

OFFICE No man goes before his time-unless the boss leaves early. (Groucho Marx)

OFFICE The brain is a wonderful organ ; it starts working the moment you get up in the morning and does not stop until you get into the office. (Robert Frost)

OFFICE What I don't like about office Christmas parties is looking for a job the next day. (Phyllis Diller)

OPINION An opinion should be the result of thought, not a substitute for it. (Jef Mallett)

OPINION If we have data, let's look at data. If all we have are opinions, let's go with mine. (Jim Barksdale)

OPINION Change your opinions, keep to your principles, change your leaves, keep intact your roots. (Victor Hugo)

OPINION Everything we hear is an opinion, not a fact. Everything we see is a perspective, not the truth. (Marcus Aurelius)

OPINION Too bad that all the people who know how to run the country are busy driving taxicabs and cutting hair. (George Burns)

OPINION   Every new opinion, at its starting, is precisely in a minority of one. (Thomas Carlyle)

OPINION   It is not best hat we should all think alike ; it is difference of opinion which makes horse races. (Mark Twain)

OPINION   It requires ages to destroy a popular opinion. (Voltaire)

OPINION   Man tends to treat all his opinions as principles. (H Agar)

OPINION   Public opinion is a compound of folly, weakness, prejudice, wrong feeling, right feeling, obstinacy, and newspaper paragraphs. (Sir Robert Peel)

OPINION   When I say 'everybody says so', I mean I say so. (Ed Howe)

OPPORTUNITY   If you're offered a seat on a rocket ship, don't ask what seat! Just get on. (Sheryl Sandberg)

OPTIMISM ☺   Optimism is the madness of insisting that all is well when we are miserable. (Voltaire)

OPTIMISM Keep your face always toward the sunshine – and shadows will fall behind you. (Walt Whitman)

OPTIMISM Look up to the sky You'll never find rainbows If you're looking down. (Charlie Chaplin)

OPTIMISM Optimism is the madness of insisting that all is well when we are miserable. (Voltaire)

OPTIMIST A pessimist is a man who thinks all women are bad. An optimist is one who hopes they are. (C Depew)

ORIGINALITY ☐   Originality is the art of remembering what you hear but forgetting where you heard it. (A Hitchcock)

OVERCONFIDENCE   Confidence is good, but overconfidence always sinks the ship. (Oscar Wilde)

OVERCONFIDENCE   In a bull market, one must avoid the error of the preening duck that quacks boastfully after a torrential rainstorm, thinking that its paddling skills have caused it to rise in the world. A right-thinking duck would instead compare its position after the downpour to that of the other ducks on the pond. (Warren Buffett)

OWNERSHIP   Any party which takes credit for the rain must not be surprised if its opponents balme it for the drought. (Dwight W Morrow)

PAIN   We must embrace pain and burn it as fuel for our journey. (Kenji Miyazawa)

PAINTING I dream my painting and I paint my dream. (Vincent van Gogh)

PARANOID   A paranoid is someone who knows a little of what is going on. (WS Burroughs)

PARENTING   You can learn many things from children. How much patience you have, for instance. (FP Jones)

PARENTING   Do not train a child to learn by force or harshness ; but direct them to it by what amuses their minds, so that you may be better able to discover with accuracy the peculiar bent of the genius of each. (Plato)

PARENTING   Never help a child with a task at which he feels he can succeed. (Maria Montessori)

PARENTING   The way we talk to our children becomes their inner voice. (Peggy O'Mara)

PARENTING ☺   One thing they never tell you about child raising is that for the rest of your life, at the drop of a hat, you are expected to know your child's name and how old he or she is. (Erma Bombeck)

PARENTING   It's not what we leave to our kids; it's what we leave within them that counts. (Valerie Sokolosky)

PARENTING   Let parents bequeath to their children not riches, but the spirit of reverence. (Plato)

PARENTING   Speak to your children as if they are the wisest, kindest, most beautiful and magical humans on earth. For what they believe is what they will become. (Brooke Hampton)

PARENTING   The reason parents no longer lead their children in the right direction is because the parents are not going that way themselves. (Kin Hubbard)

PARENTING   Before I got married, I had six theories about bringing up children, now I have six children and no theories. (John Wilmot)

PARENTING   If you want your children to be intelligent, read them fairy tales. If you want them to be more intelligent, read them more fairy tales.(Albert Einstein)

PARENTING   Never ave more children than you have car windows. (Erma Bombeck)

PARENTING   One day they will walk in your shoes, make sure they are pointed in the right direction. (LR Knost)

PARLIAMENTARIAN   Members of Congress should be compelled to wear uniforms like NASCAR drivers, so we could identify their corporate sponsors. (Caroline Baum)

PASSION   I would rather lose myself in passion than lose my passion. (J Mayol)

PASSION   If you can't figure out your purpose, figure out your passion. For your passion will lead you right into your purpose. (TD Jakes)

PASSION   One day you will eat your last meal, you will smell your last flower, you will hug your friend for the last time. You might not know it's the last time, that's why you must do everything you love with passion. (Ricky Gervais)

PASSION   What counts is not necessarily the size of the dog in the fight- it is the size of the fight in the dog. (DD Eisenhower)

PASSION   It is really hard to do a really good job on anything you don't think about in the shower. (Paul Graham)

PASSION   A man will fight harder for his interests than for his rights. (Napoleon Bonaparte)

PAST   We all grow up with the weight of history on us. Our ancestors dwell in the attics of our brains as they do in the spiralling chains of knowledge hidden in every cell of our bodies. (Shirley Abbott)

PATIENCE   Patience is not the ability to wait, but the ability to keep a good attitude while waiting. (Joyce Meyer)

PATIENCE Patience is the calm acceptance that things can happen in a different order than the one you have in mind. (David G. Allen)

PATIENCE Prayer of the modern American : "Dear God, I pray for patience. And I want it right now!" (Oren Arnold)

PATIENCE The key to everything is patience. You get the chicken by hatching the egg- not by smashing it. (Arnold Glasow)

PATRIOTISM A real patriot is the fellow who gets a parking ticket and rejoices that the system works. (Bill Vaughan)

PATRIOTISM Patriotism is as fierce as a fever, pitiless as the grave, blind as a stone and irrational as a headless hen. (Ambrose Bierce)

PEACE You cannot find peace by avoiding life. (Virginia Woolf)

PEACE All your anxiety is because of your desire for harmony. Seek disharmony, then you will gain peace. (Rumi)

PEACE Peace is not absence of conflict, it is the ability to handle conflict by peaceful means. (Ronald Reagan)

PEACE You cannot find peace by avoiding life. (Virginia Woolf)

PEOPLE Any fool knows men and women think differently at times, but the biggest difference is this. Men forget, but never forgive, women forgive, but never forget. (Robert Jordan)

PEOPLE I have learned that people will forget what you said, people will forget what you did, but people will never forget how you made them feel. (Maya Angelou)

PEOPLE   I wash my hands of those who imagine chattering to be knowledge, silence to be ignorance, and affection to be art. (K Gibran)

PEOPLE   People do not change, they are merely revealed. (Anne Enright)

PEOPLE   When dealing with people, remember you are not dealing with creatures of logic, but with creatures bristling with prejudice and motivated by pride and vanity. (Dale Carnegie)

PEOPLE   When one burns one's bridges, what a very nice fire it makes. (Dylan Thomas)

PEOPLE   When you are joyful, when you say yes to life and have fun and project positivity all around you, you become a sun in the center of every constellation, and people want to be near you. (Shannon L. Alder)

PEOPLE   A fanatic is one who can't change his mind and won't change the subject. (Winston Churchill)

PEOPLE   A fellow who is always declaring he is no fool usually has his suspicions. (R Anthony)

PEOPLE   A man who is not a Liberal at sixteen has no heart, a man who is not a Conservative at sixty has no head. (B Disraeli)

PEOPLE   Beauty is the wisdom of women. Wisdom is the beauty of men. (Chinese proverb)

PEOPLE   Better a diamond with a flaw, than a pebble without. (Confucius)

PEOPLE   Crocodiles are easy. They try to kill and eat you. People are harder. Sometimes they pretend to be your friend first. (Steve Irwin)

PEOPLE   For every credibility gap, there is
gullibility gap. (Richard Clopton)

PEOPLE   Half of the harm done in this world is
due to people who want to feel important. (T.S. Eliot)

PEOPLE   I am selfish, impatient and a little
insecure. I make mistakes, I am out of control and at
times hard to handle. But If you can't handle me at my
worst, then you sure as hell don't deserve me at my best.
(Marilyn Monroe)

PEOPLE   I love mankind ; it's people I cannot
stand. (Charles M Schulz)

PEOPLE   If you make people think they are
thinking, they will love you, but if you really make them
think, they will hate you. (DRP Marquis)

PEOPLE   It is obvious that women are smarter
than men. Think about it. Diamonds are a girl's best
friend , man's best friend is a dog. (Joan Rivers)

PEOPLE   Look out for the fellow who lets you
do all the talking. (FM Hubbard)

PEOPLE   Most people are other people. Their
thoughts are someone else's opinion., their lives a
mimicry, their passions a quotation. (Oscar WIlde)

PEOPLE   My dad once said, you would not
worry so much about what people thought of you if you
knew how seldom they did. (Dr. Phil McGraw)

PEOPLE   My own business always bores me to
death, I prefer other people's. (Oscar Wilde)

PEOPLE   People are never so ready to believe
you as when you say things in dispraise of yourself ; and

you are never so much annoyed as when they take you at your word. (WS Maugham)

PEOPLE   People only bring up your past when they are intimidated by your present. (Joubert Botha)

PEOPLE   Quiet people have the loudest minds. (Stephen Hawking)

PEOPLE   Really great men have a curious feeling that the greatness is not in them but through them. (John Ruskin)

PEOPLE   Stay away from negative people They have a problem for every solution. (Albert Einstein)

PEOPLE   Tact is the ability to describe others as they see themselves. (Abraham Lincoln)

PEOPLE   The fear of being laughed at makes cowards of us all. (Mignon McLaughlin)

PEOPLE   The greatest affliction affecting mankind is not serious mental illness – but the general uneasiness and unhappiness that is so prevalent in our society. (Carl Jung)

PEOPLE   The more I learn about people, the more I like my dog. (Mark Twain)

PEOPLE   The most precious jewels are not made of stone, but of flesh. (Robert Ludlum)

PEOPLE   The world is full of willing people, some willing to work, the rest willing to let them. (Robert Frost)

PEOPLE   Those who teach the most about humanity are not always human. (DL Hicks)

PEOPLE   Too many people spend money they have not earned to buy things they don't want o impress people they don't like. (Will Rogers)

PERFECTION   When you are a carpenter making a beautiful chest of drawers, you are not going to use a piece of plywood on the back, even though it faces the wall and nobody will see it. You will know it is there, so you are going to use a beautiful piece of wood on the back. For you to sleep well at night, the aesthetic, the quality has to be carried all the way through. (Steve Jobs)

PERFECTION   You will never achieve 100 percent if 99 percent is okay. (Will Smith)

PERSEVERANCE   It doesn't matter how slow you go, as long as you don't stop. (Confucius)

PERSEVERANCE   He who would learn to fly one day must first learn to stand and walk and run and climb and dance, one cannot fly into flying. (FW Nietzsche)

PERSEVERANCE Little strokes fell great oaks. (Benjamin Franklin)

PERSEVERANCE One of the first principles of perseverance is to know when to stop persevering. (Carolyn Wells)

PERSEVERANCE   Perseverance is not a long race, it is many short races one after another. (Walter Elliott)

PERSEVERANCE   Thankfully, perseverance is a great substitute for talent. (Steve Martin)

PERSEVERANCE   When you get to the end of your rope, tie a knot and hang on. (FD Roosevelt)

PERSISTENCE   It takes the hammer of persistence to drive the nail of success. (John Mason)

PERSISTENCE   Nothing in this world can take the place of persistence. Talent will not, nothing is more common than unsuccessful people with talent. Genius will not, unrewarded genius is almost a proverb. Education will not, the world is full of educated derelicts. Persistence and determination alone are omnipotent. The slogan 'press on' has solved and always will solve the problems of human race. (Calvin Coolidge)

PERSONALITY You can only lose something that you have, you cannot lose something that you are. (E Tolle)

PERSONALITY   If only I'd known my differentness would be an asset, then my earlier life would have been much. (Bette Midler)

PERSONALITY   I have three precious things which I hold fast and prize. The first is gentleness; the second is frugality; the third is humility, which keeps me from putting myself before others. Be gentle and you can be bold; be frugal and you can be liberal; avoid putting yourself before others and you can become a leader among men. (Lao Tzu)

PERSPCTIVE   Those who danced were thought to be insane by those who could not hear the music. (Nietzsche)

PERSPECTIVE   Those who danced were thought to be quite insane by those who could not hear the music. (Angela Monet)

PERSPECTIVE   A man sees in the world what he carries in his heart.   (Goethe)

PERSPECTIVE   Absence may or may not make the heart grow fonder, but it certainly freshens the eye. (Stephen King)

PERSPECTIVE   If you only have a hammer, you tend to see every problem as a nail. (Abe Lincoln)

PERSPECTIVE   It is not always a change of scenery needed to make life better. Sometimes it simply requires opening your eyes. (R.E.Goodrich)

PERSPECTIVE   The real voyage of discovery consists not in seeking new lands, but in seeing with new eyes. (Marcel Proust)

PERSPECTIVE   When I was a boy of fourteen, my father was so ignorant I could hardly stand to have the old man around. But when I got to be twenty-one, I was astonished t how much he had learned in seven years. (Mark Twain)

PERSPECTIVE   You never really understand a person until you consider things from his point of view, until you climb inside of his skin and walk around in it. (Harper Lee)

PERSUASION   Persuasion occurs when trust & confidence meet belief, risk, tolerance & safety. (J.Gitomer)

PERSUASION   Since 95 percent of the people are imitators and only 5 percent initiators, people are persuaded more by the actions of others than by any proof we can offer. (Robert B. Cialdini)

PESSIMISM   The person who says it cannot be done should not interrupt the person who is doing it. (Chinese proverb)

PESSIMIST ☺   A pessimist is a man who thinks everybody is as nasty as himself, and hates them for it. (GB Shaw)

PESSIMIST I have never seen a monument erected to a pessimist. (Paul Harvey)

PESSIMIST The nice part about being a pessimist is that you are constantly being either proven right or pleasantly surprised.(George Will)

PESSIMIST There is no sadder sight than a young pessimist. (Mark Twain)

PET I tend to be suspicious of people whose love of animals is exaggerated, they are often frustrated in their relationships with humans. (Camilla Koffler)

PHILANTHROPY Billions are wasted on ineffective philanthropy. Philanthropy is decades behind business in applying rigorous thinking to the use of money. (Michael Porter)

PHILOSOPHY Philosophy is common sense with big words. (James Madison)

PHOTO Today everything exists to end in a photograph. (Susan Sontag)

PLANNING Give me six hours to chop down a tree and I will spend the first hour sharpening the axe. (A Lincoln)

PLANNING You don't always need a plan. Sometimes you just need to breathe, trust, let go, and see what happens. (Mandy Hale)

POETRY Genuine poetry can communicate before it is understood. (TS Eliot)

POETRY He who draws noble delights from sentiments of poetry is a true poet, though he has never written a line in all his life. (George Sand)

POETRY   Poets are always taking the weather so personally. They are always sticking their emotions in things that have no emotions. (JD Salinger)

POLITENESS   A kindly tongue is the lodestone of the hearts of men. It is the bread of the spirit, it clotheth the words with meaning, it is the fountain of the light of wisdom and understanding. (Bahaullah)

POLITENESS ☺   Politeness is the art of choosing among one's real thoughts. (Abel Stevens)

POLITICIAN   I once said cynically of a politician, "He will doublecross that bridge when he comes to it." (Oscar Levant)

POLITICIAN   A politician divides mankind into two classes- tools and enemies. (FW Nietzsche)

POLITICIAN   A politician is an animal who can sit on a fence and yet keep both ears to the ground. (American proverb)

POLITICS I always cheer up immensely if an attack is particularly wounding because I think, well, if they attack one personally, it means they have not a single political argument left. (M Thatcher)

POLITICS I am not a consensus politician. I am a conviction politician. (M Thatcher)

POLITICS There are no morals in politics ; there is only expedience. A scoundrel may be of use to us just because he is a scoundrel. (V Lenin)

POLITICS ☺   A promising young man should go into politics so that he can go on promising for the rest of his life. (Robert Byrne)

POLITICS A politician needs the ability to foretell what is going to happen tomorrow, next week, next month, and next year. And to have the ability afterwards to explain why it did not happen. (Winston Churchill)

POLITICS An honest politician is one who, when he is bought, will stay bought. (Simon Cameron)

POLITICS Corrupt politicians make the other ten percent look bad. (Henry Kissinger)

POLITICS In order to become the master, the politician poses as the servant. (Charles de Gaulle)

POLITICS In politics, nothing happens by accident. If it happens, you can bet it was planned that way. (FD Roosevelt)

POLITICS Just because you do not take an interest in politics does not mean politics won't take an interest in you. (Pericles)

POLITICS Our great democracies still tend to think that a stupid man is more likely to be honest than a clever man, and our politicians take advantage of this prejudice by pretending to be even more stupid than nature made them. (B Russell)

POLITICS Politics has become so expensive that it takes a lot of money even to be defeated. (Will Rogers)

POLITICS Politics is the art of looking for trouble, finding it, misdiagnosing it, and then misapplying the wrong remedies. (Groucho Marx)

POLITICS Politics is the art of postponing decisions until they are no longer relevant. (Henri Queuille)

POLITICS   Politics is the gentle art of getting votes from the poor and campaign funds from the rich, by promising to protect each from the other. (Oscar Ameringer)

POLITICS   Politics is war without blood, while war is politics with blood.   (Mao Tse-tung)

POLITICS   Politics, as a practice, whatever its professions, has always been the systematic organization of hatreds. (Henry Adams)

POLITICS   Politics, it seems to me, for years, or all too long, has been concerned with right or left instead of right or wrong. (Richard Armour)

POLITICS   Since a politician never believes what he says, he is surprised when others believe him. (Charles de Gaulle)

POLITICS   The first lesson of economics is scarcity. The first lesson of politics is to disregard the first lesson of economics. (Thomas Sowell)

POLITICS   The magician and the politicians have much in common : they both have to draw our attention away from what they are really doing.(Ben Okri)

POLITICS   The most successful politician is he who says what the people are thinking most often in the loudest voice. (Theodore Roosevelt)

POLITICS   When buying and selling are controlled by legislation, the first things to be bought and sold are legislators. (PJ O'Rourke)

POLITICS   When they call the roll in the Senate, the senators do not know whether to answer 'present' or 'not guilty'. (Theodore Roosevelt)

POLITICS   You campaign in poetry. You govern in prose.
(Mario Cuomo)

POLLUTION   People don't pollute because
they like polluting. They do it because it's a cheaper way of
producing something else. (Ronald Coase)

POOR   The poor are no less rational than anybody
else- quite the contrary. They have to be sophisticated
economists just to survive. (A Banerjee and E Duflo)

POSSESSION   The way to love anything is to realize
that it might be lost. (GK Chesterton)

POTENTIAL   Big jobs usually go to the
men who prove their ability to outgrow small ones. (T
Roosevelt)

POTENTIAL   We have more possibilities available
in each moment than we realize. (Thich Nhat Hanh)

POVERTY There are people in the world so hungry, that
God cannot appear to them except in the form of bread.
(Mahatma Gandhi)

POVERTY The best way to help the poor is not to
become one of them. (Lang Hancock)

POVERTY There were times my pants were so thin that I
could sit on a dime and tell if it were heads or tails.
(Spencer Tracy)

POWER   Aerodynamically the bumblebee should not
be able to fly, but the bumblebee does not know that so it
goes on flying anyway. (Mary Kay Ash)

POWER   Power remains strong when it remains in the
dark; exposed to the sunlight it begins to evaporate.
(Samuel P. Huntington)

POWER   Power remains strong when it remains in the dark; exposed to the sunlight it begins to evaporate. (Samuel P. Huntington)

POWER   There is a lure in power. It can get into a man's blood just as gambling and lust for money have been known to do. (Harry S. Truman)

POWER   He who wishes to be obeyed must know how to command. (Machiavelli)

POWER   Nearly all men can stand adversity, but if you want to test a man's character, give him power. (Abe Lincoln)

POWER   The attempt to combine wisdom and power has only rarely been successful and then only for a short while. (Albert Einstein)

POWER   The most common way people give up their power is by thinking they don't have any. (Alice Walker)

POWER   The new source of power is not money in the hands of the few but information in the hands of many. (John Naisbitt)

POWER   What it lies in our power to do, it lies in our power not to do. (Aristotle)

PRAISE   Few things offer a greater return on less investment than praise. (Bill Walsh)

PRAISE   Praise out of season, or tactlessly bestowed, can freeze the heart as much as blame. (Pearl S. Buck)

PRAISE   Appreciation can make a day, even change a life. Your willingness to put it into words is all that is necessary. (Margaret Cousins)

PRAISE   Appreciation is a wonderful thing: It makes what is excellent in others belong to us as well. (Voltaire)

PRAISE   If you see something beautiful in someone, speak it. (Ruthie Lindsey)

PRAISE   Most people don't know how AWESOME they are, until you tell them. Be sure to tell them. (Kelvin Ringold)

PREJUDICE   Prejudice is a great time saver. You can form opinions without having to get the facts. (EB White)

PRESS   A free press can be good or bad, but, most certainly, without freedom a press will never be anything but bad. (Albert Camus)

PREVENTION   A danger foreseen is half-avoided. (Cheyenne)

PRIDE   The trouble with some self-made men is that they insist on giving everybody else the recipe. (Maurice Seitter)

PRINCIPLE   To become good at anything you have to know how to apply basic principles. To become great at it, you have to know when to violate those principles. (Garry Kasparov)

PRINCIPLEIn matters of style, swim with the current, in matters of principle, stand like a rock. (Thomas Jefferson)

PRIVACY   Privacy is dead, and social media holds the smoking gun. (Pete Cashmore)

PROBLEM There is no such thing as a problem without a gift for you in its hands. You seek problems because you need their gifts. (Richard Bach)

PROBLEM A solved problem creates two new problems, and the best prescription for happy living is not to solve any more problems than you have to. (Russell Baker)

PROFESSION   The price one pays for pursuing any profession or calling is an intimate knowledge of its ugly side. (James Baldwin)

PROGRESS   Healthy discontent is the prelude to progress. (MK Gandhi)

PROMISE Those that are most slow in making a promise are the most faithful in the performance of it. (Jean-Jacques Rousseau)

PROPERTY Buy land, they are not making it anymore. (Mark Twain)

PROPERTY Don't wait to buy real estate, buy real estate and wait. (Will Rogers)

PROPERTY The best time to buy a home is always five years ago. (Ray Brown)

PROSPERITY   Prosperity is only an instrument to be used, not a deity to be worshipped. (Calvin Coolidge)

PROSTITUTION   My method is basically the same as Masters and Johnson, only they charge thousands of dollars and it is called therapy. I charge fifty dollars and it is called prostitution. (Xaviera Hollander)

QUEST   Maybe you are searching among the branches, for what only appears in the roots. (Rumi)

QUEST   He who would search for pearls must dive below. (John Dryden)

QUEST   The ultimate search engine would basically understand everything in the world, and it would always give you the right thing. And we are a long long way from that. (Larry Page)

QUEST   When you go in search of honey you must expect to be stung by bees. (J Joubert)

RAIN   Rain is grace ; rain is the sky descending to the earth ; without rain, there would be no life. (John Updike)

RAIN   Some people walk in the rain, others just get wet. (Roger Miller)

RAIN   The best thing one can do when it's raining is to let it rain. (HW Longfellow)

READING We should not teach great books, we should teach a love of reading. (BF Skinner)

READING I am part of all that I have read. (John Kieran)

READING I took a speed-reading course and read War and Peace in twenty minutes. It involves Russia. (Woody Allen)

READING If you believe everything you read, better not read. (Japanese proverb)

READING It is what you read when you don't have to that determines who you will be when you can't help it. (Oscar Wilde)

READING Reading gives us someplace to go when we have to tay where we are. (Mason Cooley)

READING Reading is sometimes an ingenious device for avoiding thought. (Arthur Helps)

READING Reading is to the mind what exercise is to the body. (Sir Richard Steele)

READING Reading should not be presented to children as a chore, a duty. It should be offered as a gift. (Charles Scribner, Jr.)

READING Reading without reflecting is like eating without digesting. (Edmund Burke)

READING The art of reading is to skip judiciously. (PG Hamerton)

READING The greatest gift is a passion for reading. It is cheap, it consoles, it distracts, it excites, it gives you the knowledge of the world and experience of a wide kind. It is moral illumination. (Elizabeth Hardwick)

READING The man who does not read good books has no advantage over the man who cannot read them. (Mark Twain)

READING The most important thing is to read as much as you can, like I did. It will give you an understanding of what makes good writing and it will enlarge your vocabulary. (JK Rowlings)

READING Verses which do not teach men new and moving truths do not deserve to be read. (Voltaire)

READING We read every day, with astonishment, things which we see every day, without surprise. (Earl of Chesterfield)

READING We read to say that we have read. (Charles Lamb)

REASON An explanation of cause is not a justification by reason. (CS Lewis)

REASON Human reason is a very convenient and accommodating instrument and works only in the circle set for it by interest, partiality and prejudice. (Sri Aurindo)

REASON   People are usually more convinced by reasons they discovered themselves than by those found by others. (Blaise Pascal)

RECRUITMENT   Hire character. Train skill. (Peter Schultz)

REFLECTION   By non-doing, all doing becomes possible. (Lao Tsu)

RELATION Some people are going to leave, but that is not the end of your story. That is the end of their part in your story. (Faraaz Kazi)

RELATIONS   Could a greater miracle take place than for us to look through each other's eyes for an instant? (HD Thoreau)

RELATIONSHIP   Don't be reckless with other people's hearts. Don't put up with people who are reckless with yours. (Mary Schmich)

RELATIONSHIP   Indifference is expensive. Hostility is unaffordable. Trust is priceless. It's all about Relationships. (Ted Rubin)

RELATIONSHIP   Open your hands if you want to be held. (Rumi)

RELATIONSHIP   To handle yourself, use your head; to handle others, use your heart. (Eleanor Roosevelt)

RELATIONSHIP   We are all full of weakness and errors; let us mutually pardon each other our follies, it is the first law of nature. (Voltaire)

RELATIONSHIP   When we honestly ask ourselves which person in our lives means the most to us, we often find that it is those who, instead of giving advice, solutions, or cures, have chosen rather to share our pain and touch our wounds with a warm and tender hand. (Henri Nouwen)

RELATIONSHIP   Don't be reckless with other people's hearts. Don't put up with people who are reckless with yours. (Mary Schmich)

RELATIONSHIP   Don't judge me until you know me. Don't underestimate me until you challenge me. Don't talk about me until you talk to me. (Scott Eddy)

RELATIONSHIP   If you're absent during my struggle, don't expect to be present during my success. (Will Smith)

RELATIONSHIP   Never wish them pain. That's not who you are. If they caused you pain, they must have pain inside. Wish them healing. (Najwa Zebian)

RELATIONSHIP   The Japanese have a word for it. It's judo- the art of conquering by yielding. The Western equivalent of judo is 'yes, dear'. (JP McEvoy)

RELATIONSHIP   Understanding is the first step to acceptance, and only with acceptance can there be recovery. (J.K. Rowling)

RELATIVE With a relation, eat and drink, but conduct no business with him. (Greek proverb)

RELATIVITY   When people see some things as beautiful, other things become ugly. When people see some things as good, other things become bad. (Lao Tzu)

RELAXATION   Just because technology makes it possible to be always available, does not mean you should be. (JL Stoner)

RELIGION I belong to no religion. My religion is love. Every heart is my temple. (Rumi)

RELIGION Religion is the opium of the masses. (Karl Marx)

RELIGION ☺ The only difference between a cult and a religion is the amount of real estate they own. (Frank Zappa)

RELIGION Religion is regarded by the common people as true, by the wise as false, and by rulers as useful. (Seneca)

RELIGION We have just enough religion to make us hate, but not enough to make us love one another. (J Swift)

RESEARCH Research is formalised curiosity. It is poking and prying with a purpose. (ZN Hurston)

RESILIENCE At any given moment you have the power to say this is not how the story is going to end. (Christine M. Miller)

 RESILIENCE The greatest glory in living lies not in never falling, but in rising every time we fall. (RW Emerson)

RESOLUTION Many years ago, I resolved never to bother with New Year's resolutions, and I have stuck with it ever since. (Dave Beard)

RESOURCES The meek shall inherit the earth but not its mineral rights. (J.Paul Getty)

RESPECT You should never be surprised when someone treats you with respect. You should expect it. (Sarah Dessen)

RESPECT Respect for ourselves guides our morals, respect for others guides our manners. (L Sterne)

REST   Almost everything will work again if you unplug it for a few minutes, including you. (Anne Lamott)

RESULT   What I am looking for is a blessing not in disguise. (Jerome K Jerome)

RETIREMENT   When a man retires and time is no longer a matter of urgent importance, his colleagues generally present him with a watch. (RC Sherriff)

REVIEW   I never read a book before reviewing it. It prejudices me so. (Sydney Smith)

REVOLUTION   Revolution is the festival of the oppressed. (Germaine Greer)

RICH   I am so happy to be rich, I am willing to take all the consequences. (Howard Abramson)

RICH   I think everybody should get rich and famous and do everything they ever dreamed of so they can see that it is not the answer. (Jim Carrey)

RICH   I would like to be rich enough so that I could throw soap away after the letters are worn off. (Andy Rooney)

RICH   I would like to live like a poor man with lots of money. (Pablo Picasso)

RICH   No one has ever achieved financial success by constantly spending all they have in order to deceive others into believing they are rich. (Edmond Mbiaka)

RICH   Sometimes the pilgrimage from rags to riches is a journey from rage to wretchedness. (RM Huber)

RICH   The rich never feel so good as when they are speaking of their possessions as responsibilities. (Robert Lynd)

RICH   The rich would have to eat money, but luckily the poor provide food. (Russian Proverb)

RICH   The suffering of the rich is among the sweetest pleasures of the poor. (RM Huber)

RIGHT   The minute you settle for less than you deserve, you get even less than you settled for. (M Dowd)

RIGHTS   If some people got their rights they would complain of being deprived of their wrongs. (Oliver Heford)

RIGHTS   What men value in this world is not rights but privileges. (HL Mencken)

RIOT   A riot is the language of unheard. (MLK Jr.)

RISK   And the day came when the risk to remain tight in a bud was more painful than the risk it took to blossom. (Anais Nin)

RISK $ The difference between risk and uncertainty is that you can attach a probability to risk but not to uncertainty. (Frank Knight)

RISK   I backed the right horse, and then the wrong horse went and won. (Henry Herman)

RISK   Only those who will risk going too far can possibly find out how far one can go. (TS Eliot)

RISK   Virtually, every important action in life involves educated guesswork. Too few chances reliably translate into too few victories. (Thomas W. Hazlett)

RISK   We demand rigidly defined areas of doubt and uncertainty. (Douglas Adams)

RISK   You can't leave a footprint that lasts if you are always walking on tiptoe. (Marion C.Blakey)

ROBOT   I visualize a time when we will be to robots what dogs are to humans, and I am rooting for the machines. (Claude Shannon)

ROMANCE The very essence of romance is uncertainty. (Oscar Wilde)

RUDENESS   Rudeness is the weak person's imitation of strength. (Eric Hoffer)

RUMOUR When the eagles are silent, the parrots begin to jabber. (Winston Churchill)

RUMOUR   Nobody believes a rumour here in Washington until it is officially denied. (E Cheyfitz)

RUNNING   If you don't think you were born to run you're not only denying history. You're denying who you are. (Christopher McDougall)

SADNESS You cannot prevent the birds of sadness from passing over your head, but you can prevent their making a nest in your hair. (Chinese proverb)

SALARY   The three most harmful addictions are heroin, carbohydrates and a monthly salary. (NM Taleb)

SATIRE   Satire does not look pretty upon a tombstone. (Charles Lamb)

SATIRE   Deep breaths are very helpful at shallow parties. (Barbara Walters)

SATIRE   Every time Congress makes a joke it's law, and every time they make a law it's a joke. (Will Rogers)

SATIRE   It would be a terrific innovation if you could get your mind to stretch a little further than the next wisecrack. (K Hepburn)

SATIRE   My generation is not strong. My grandfather fought in WW II. I had a panic attack during the series finale of Breaking Bad. (Matt Donaher)

SATIRE   My Lord. It is too much, and not enough. Jacqueline Carey)

SATIRE   The four of the most beautiful words there are : I told you so. (Gore Vidal)

SATIRE   If living conditions don't stop improving in the country, we are going to run out of humble beginnings for our great men. (RP Askue)

SCIENCE ☺Photons have mass? I did not even know they were catholic. (Woody Allen)

SECRET ☺ We, women, talk too much, but even then, we don't tell half what we know. (Nancy Astor)

SECRET   Loose lips sink big ships. (Russian proverb)

SECRET   There are no secrets better kept than the secrets everybody guesses. (GB Shaw)

SEER   The best of seers is he who guesses well. (Euripides)

SELF   The butterfly does not look back at the caterpillar in shame, just as you should not look back at your past in shame. Your past was part of your own transformation. (Anthony Gucciardi)

SELF   Be gentle with yourself. You are a child of the universe, no less

SELF   Because one believes in oneself, one doesn't try to convince others. Because one is content with oneself, one doesn't need others' approval. Because one accepts oneself, the whole world accepts him or her. (Lao Tzu)

SELF   Better keep yourself clean and bright ; you are the window through which you must see the world. (GB Shaw)

SELF   I don't entirely approve of some of the things I have done, or am, or have been. But I am me. (Elizabeth Taylor)

SELF   If it's never our fault, we can't take responsibility for it. If we can't take responsibility for it, we will always be its victim. (Richard Bach)

SELF   Not until we are lost do we begin to find ourselves. (Thoreau)

SELF   Nothing can dim the light that shines from within. (Maya Angelou)

SELF   Self-compassion is positively associated with virtually every desirable outcome in terms of psychological well-being. (Dr. Dan Siegel)

SELF   The best years of your life are the ones in which you decide your problems are your own. You do not blame them on your mother, the ecology, or the president. You realize that you control your own destiny. (Albert Ellis)

SELF   The world tells us to be our best selves, to be amazing, to be an inspiration. Sometimes, it's nice to just BE. (Jessica de la Davies)

SELF   Those who are unaware they are walking in darkness will never seek the light. (Bruce Lee)

SELF   Your whole idea about yourself is borrowed – borrowed from those who have no idea of who they are themselves. (Osho)

SELF   I count him braver who overcomes his desires than him who conquers his enemies, for the hardest victory is over self. (Aristotle)

SELF   Knowing your own darkness is the best method for dealing with the darknesses of other people. (Carl Jung)

SELF   Self-esteem is not a luxury; it is a profound spiritual need. (Nathaniel Branden)

SELF   But he who is truly wise, always sees the absolute Self. Celebrated, he is not delighted. Spurned, he is not angry. (Ashtavakra)

SELF   Don't let the noise of others' opinions drown out your own inner voice. (Steve Jobs)

SELF   It is hard to believe that a man is telling the truth when you know that you would lie if you were in his place. (HL Mencken)

SELF   Learning to ignore things is one of the greatest paths to inner peace. (Robert J.Sawyer)

SELF   Never be afraid to laugh at yourself, after all, you could be missing out on the joke of the century. (Barry Humphries)

SELF   One advantage of talking to yourself is that you know at least somebody is listening. (FP Jones)

SELF   Our business in life is not to get ahead of others, but to get ahead of ourselves-to break our own records, to outstrip our yesterday by our today. (Stewart B. Johnson)

SELF   Our lives only improve when we are willing to take chances and the first and the most difficult risk we can take is to be honest with ourselves. (Walter Anderson)

SELF   Rather than being your thoughts and emotions, be the awareness behind them. (Eckhart Tolle)

SELF   The days you are most uncomfortable are the days you learn the most about yourself. (Mary L. Bean)

SELF   The first thing you have to know is yourself. A man who knows himself can step outside himself and watch his own reactions like an observer. (Adam Smith)

SELF   There is as much difference between us and ourselves as between us and others. (Montaigne)

SELF   Treat those who are good with goodness, and also treat those who are not good with goodness. Thus goodness is attained. Be honest to those who are honest, and be also honest to those who are not honest. Thus honesty is attained. (Lao Tzu)

SELF   When we are no longer able to change a situation, we are challenged to change ourselves. (Viktor Frankl)

SELF   Who are we but the stories we tell ourselves, about ourselves, and believe?" (Scott Turow)

SELF   Your most important sale in life is to sell yourself to yourself. (Maxwell Maltz)

SELF-AWARENESS   The quality of your life will be determined by the quality of the questions you ask yourself. (Tony Robbins)

SELFISH   People aren't against you; they are for themselves. (Caroline Zelonka)

SELF-RESPECT   If I am not good to myself, how can I expect anyone else to be good to me? (Maya Angelou)

SELLING   A man without a smiling face must not open a shop. (Chinese proverb)

SELLING   Every sale has five basic obstacles : no need, no money, no hurry, no desire, no trust. (Zig Ziglar)

SELLING   He would sell even his share of the sun. (Italian proverb)

SELLING   The best salesman we ever heard of was the one who sold two milking machines to a farmer who had only one cow. Then this salesman helped finance the deal by taking the cow as down payment on the two milking machines. (Herbert V. Prochnow)

SELLING   There is no such thing as soft-sell or hard-sell. There is only smart-sell and stupid-sell.(Charles Brower)

SELLING   When a man is trying to sell you something, don't imagine that he is that polite all the time. (EW Howe)

SELLING   When you are skinning your customers, you should leave some skin on to grow so that you can skin them again. (Nikita Khrushchev)

SENATE   When they call the roll in the Senate, the Senators do not know whether to answer 'Present' or 'Not Guilty'. (Theodore Roosevelt)

SERVICE   To give real service you must add something which cannot be bought or measured with money, and that is sincerity and integrity. (D Adams)

SEX   Everything in the world is about sex except sex. Sex is about power.   (Oscar Wilde)

SEX   Women fake orgasms and men fake finances. (Suze Orman)

SEXY ☺   Sex appeal is fifty percent what you have got and fifty percent what people think you have got. (Sophia Loren)

SHARING You are forgiven for your happiness and your successes only if you generously consent to share them. (Albert Camus)

SHOPPING Don't a fellow feel good after he gets out of a store where he nearly bought something? (FM Hubbard)

SHOPPING Thus, in the future, instead of buying bananas in a grocery store,, you could go pick them off a tree in a virtual jungle. (Y Fukushima)

SILENCE   Silence is the sleep that nourishes wisdom. (Francis Bacon)

SILENCE ☺Blessed is the man who, having nothing to say, abstains from giving us worthy evidence of the fact. (George Eliot)

SILENCE   Listen to silence. It has so much to say. (Rumi)

SILENCE   Silence is the most perfect expression of scorn. (GB Shaw)

SILENCE   So, if you are too tired to speak, sit next to me, because I, too, am fluent in silence. (R Arnold)

SIMPLICITY   That has been one of my mantras- focus and simplicity. Simple can be harder than complex, you have to work hard to get your thinking clean to make it simple. (Steve Jobs)

SIMPLICITY   It is very simple to be happy, but it is very difficult to be simple. (R Tagore)

SIMPLICITY   I am convinced that there can be luxury in simplicity. (Jil Sander)

SKEPTICISM   Skepticism   is   hedge   against vulnerability. (CT Samuels)

SLANDER I always cheer up immensely if an attack is particularly wounding because I think, well, if they attack one personally, it means they have not a single political argument left. (Margaret Thatcher)

SLANDER If you must slander someonedon't speak it but write it- write it in the sand, near the water's edge. (Napoleon Hill)

SLEEP   Sleep is the single most effective thing we can do to reset our brain and body health each day — Mother Nature's best effort yet at contra-death. (Matthew Walker)

SLEEP   The shorter your sleep, the shorter your life. The leading causes of disease and death in developed nations—diseases that are crippling health-care systems, such as heart disease, obesity, dementia, diabetes, and cancer—all have recognized causal links to a lack of sleep. (Matthew Walker)

SLEEP ☺   Sleep is my favourite thing in the world. It is the reason I get up in the morning. (Ross Smith)

SLEEP   The physical and mental impairments caused by one night of bad sleep dwarf those caused by an equivalent absence of food or exercise. (Matthew Walker)

SMART   I am so clever that sometimes I don't understand a single word of what I am saying. (Oscar Wilde)

SMARTNESS   Admire a little ship, but put your cargo in a big one. (Hesiod)

SMARTNESS   Never insult an alligator until after you have crossed the river. (Cordell Hull)

SMILE   If you're concerned with how you look when you smile, you're doing it wrong. (Connor Chalfant)

SMILE   Smiling is the best way to face every problem, to crush every fear and to hide every pain. (Will Smith)

SOCIALISM   The problem with socialism is that you eventually run out of other people's money. (M Thatcher)

SOCIETY   The most perfect political community is one in which the middle class is in control, and outnumbers both at the other classes. (Aristotle)

SOCIETY   When the gap between ideal and real becomes too wide, the system breaks down. (Barbara Tuchman)

SOCIETY   Each generation imagines itself to be more intelligent than the one that went before it , and wiser than the one that comes after it. (George Orwell)

SOCIETY   If you want good service, serve yourself. (Spanish proverb)

SOCIETY   It is one of nature's ways that we often feel closer to distant generations than to the generation immediately preceding us. (Igor Stravinsky)

SOCIETY   No man is an island, entire of itself ; every man is a piece of the continent, a part of the main. (John Donne)

SOCIETY   No matter how thin you slice it, it is still baloney. (AE Smith)

SOCIETY   Nothing makes you more tolerant of a neighbour's noisy party than being there. (FP Jones)

SOCIETY   Our scientific power has outrun our spiritual power. We have guided missiles and misguided men. (Martin Luther King Jr.)

SOCIETY   Society exists only as a mental concept, in the real world there are only individuals. (Oscar Wilde)

SOCIETY   The radical of one country is the conservative of the next. The radical invents the views. When he has worn them out the conservative adopts them. (Mark Twain)

SOCIETY   The trouble with the profit system has always been that it was highly unprofitable to most people. (EB White)

SOCIETY   There is always more misery among the lower classes than there is humanity in the higher. (Victor Hugo)

SOCIETY   Whenever two people meet there are really six people present. There is each man as he sees himself, each man as the other person sees him, and each man as he really is. (William James)

SOCIETY   Whenever you find yourself on the side of the majority, it is time to pause and reflect. (Mark Twain)

SOCIETY The saddest aspect of life right now is that science gathers knowledge faster than society gathers wisdom. (Isaac Asimov)

SOLITUDE   The best remedy for those who are afraid, lonely or unhappy is to go outside, somewhere where they can be quiet, alone with the heavens, nature and God. As long as this exists, and it certainly always will, then there will be comfort for every sorrow, whatever the circumstances may be. (Anne Frank)

SOLITUDE All of humanity's problems stem from man's inability to sit quietly in a room alone. (Blaise Pascal)

SOLITUDE Be alone, that is the secret of invention; be alone, that is when ideas are born. (Nikola Tesla)

SOLITUDE I need solitude in my life as I need food and drink and the laughter of little children. Extravagant though it may sound, solitude is the filter of my soul. It nourishes me and rejuvenates me. Left alone, I discovered that I keep myself good company. (Sophia Loren)

SORROW The deeper sorrow carves into your being the more joy you can contain. (Khalil Gibran)

SOUL   You can't lie to your soul. (Irvine Welsh)

SOUL   Do not sell your soul in exchange of anything, this is the only thing you have brought into this world and the only thing you can take back. (Rumi)

SPECIALIZATION Specialization is for insects. (Robert Heinlein)

SPEECH   It usually takes me more than three weeks to prepare a good impromptu speech. (Mark Twain)

SPEECH   A speech is a solemn responsibility The man who makes a bad thirty-minute speech to two hundred people wastes only a half hour of his own time. But he wastes one hundred hours of the audience's time- more than four days which should be a hanging offence. (JL Jones)

SPEECH   Once you get people laughing, they are listening and you can tell them almost anything. (Herbert Gardner)

SPEECH   Oratory is the power to talk people out of their sober and natural opinions. (Paul Chatfield)

SPEECH   Do not talk to me of Archimedes' lever. He was an absent-minded person with a mathematical imagination. Mathematics command my respect, but I have no use for engines. Give me the right word and the right accent and I will move the world. (Joseph Conrad)

SPIRIT   In everyone's life at some time, our inner fire goes out. It is then burst into flame by an encounter with another human being. We should all be thankful for those people who rekindle the inner spirit. (Albert Schweltzer)

SPORTS   Like books, sports give people a sense of having lived other lives, of taking part in other people's victories. And defeats. (Phil Knight)

STARTUP   In a startup company, you basically throw out all assumptions every three weeks. (WL Phelps)

STATESMAN   The difference between a politician and a statesman is : a politician thinks of the next election and a statesman thinks of the next generation. (JF Clarke)

STATISTICS   There are three types of lies
— lies, damn lies, and statistics. (Benjamin Disraeli)

STATUS   No matter the economy of the jungle.
The lion will never eat grass. (African proverb)

STORY   A story isn't a charcoal sketch, where
every stroke lies on the surface to be seen. It's an oil
painting, filled with layers that the author must uncover
so carefully to show its beauty. (AA Rhodes)

STORY   Stories never really end, even if the
books like to pretend they do. Stories always go on. They
don't end on the last page, any more than they begin on
the first page. (C Funke)

STORY   Storytelling reveals meaning without
committing the error of defining it. (Hannah Arendt)

STORY   The universe is made of stories, not
atoms. (Muriel Rukeyser)

STRATEGY There are some things one can only achieve
by a deliberate leap in the opposite direction. (Franz
Kafka)

STRENGTH   There are two ways of
exerting one's strength : one is pushing down, the other is
pulling up. (BT Washington)

STRENGTH   The world breaks everyone, and
afterward, some are strong at the broken places. (Ernest
Hemingway)

STRESS   It is not the load that breaks you down, it is
the way you carry it. (Lou Holtz)

STRESS   A good laugh and a long sleep are the
two best cures for anything. (Irish proverb)

STRESS   Resistance creates suffering. Stress happens when your mind resists what is..The only problem in your life is your mind's resistance to life as it unfolds. (Dan Millman)

STRUGGLE   It is not the mountains ahead to climb that wear you out, it is the pebble in your stone. (M Ali)

STRUGGLEI am a self-made man, but I think if I had to do it over again, I'd call in someone else. (Roland Young)

STUPIDITY ☺   Genius has limitations ; stupidity is boundless. (Albert Einstein)

STYLE   Style is a way to say who you are without having to speak. (Rachel Zoe)

SUCCESS   Don't let a mad world tell you that success is anything other than a successful present moment. (Eckhart Tolle)

SUCCESS   Success will not lower its standard to us. We must raise our standard to success. (John DiJulius)

SUCCESS   There is only one success - to be able to spend your life in your own way. (Christopher Morley)

SUCCESS Success and failure are equally disastrous. (Tennessee Williams)

SUCCESS To do more for the world than the world does for you that is success. (Henry Ford)

SUCCESS ☺   I could not wait for success, si I went ahead without it. (Jonathan Miller)

SUCCESS   If you wish to succeed in life, make perseverance your bosom friend, experience your wise counselor, caution your elder brother and hope your guardian genius. (Jospeh Addison)

SUCCESS   Ambition is the path to success. Persistence is the vehicle you arrive in. (Bill Eardley)

SUCCESS   Define success on your own terms, achieve it by your own rules, and build a life you're proud to live. (Anne Sweeney)

SUCCESS   Do not hold the delusion that your advancement is accomplished by crushing others. (Cicero)

SUCCESS   Great things are not done by impulse, but by a series of small things brought together. (George Eliot)

SUCCESS   I can give you a six-word formula for success: "Think things through - then follow through." (Edward Rickenbacker)

SUCCESS   I have had all the disadvantages required for success. (Larry Ellison)

SUCCESS   If you are lucky enough to be different, don't ever change. (Taylor Swift)

SUCCESS   If you start off being afraid of failure, you will end up also fearing success because then you will have something to lose. (Luis Spota)

SUCCESS   It is not the mountain we conquer, but ourselves. (Sir Edmund Hillary)

SUCCESS   It is not the time in the ring that wins a fight, but the work at 4.30 a.m., with no one watching that makes me a champion. (Muhammed Ali)

SUCCESS   Most people will never accomplish the long term great because they settle for the short term good. (Reg Saddler)

SUCCESS   Some people dream of success, while others wake up and work hard at it. (Mark Zuckerberg)

SUCCESS   Success is having to worry about every damn thing in the world, except money. (Johnny Cash)

SUCCESS   Success is often the result of taking a misstep in the right direction. (Al Bernstein)

SUCCESS   The man on top of the mountain didn't fall there. (Vince Lombardi)

SUCCESS   There is nothing that fails like success. (GK Chesterton)

SUCCESS   Thing PIG – that's my motto. P stands for Persistence, I stands for Integirty, and G stands for Guts. These are the ingredients for a successful business and a successful life. (Linda Chandler)

SUCCESS   True success is overcoming the fear of being unsuccessful. (Paul Sweeney)

SUFFERING   Suffering is humbling. It pays to know how to get your butt kicked. (Christopher McDougall)

SUPPLY   Give a man a fish and he will eat for a day. Teach a man to fish and he will eat for a lifetime. Teach a man to create an artificial shortage of fish and he will eat steak. (Jay Leno)

TALENT   Women are the largest untapped reservoir of talent in the world. (Hillary Clinton)

TALENT   Mediocrity knows nothing higher than itself, but talent instantly recognises genius. (Arthur Conan Doyle)

TALENT   You are only given a little spark of madness. You must not lose it. (Robin Williams)

TAX   We contend that for a nation to try to tax itself into prosperity is like a man standing in a bucket and trying to lift himself up by the handle. (W Churchill)

TAX   I am spending a year dead for tax reasons. (D Adams)

TAX   The reward of energy, enterprise and thrift is taxes. (A Dickinson)

TAX   The way taxes are, you might as well marry for love. (Bob Hope)

TAX   We contend that for a nation to try to tax itself into prosperity is like a man standing in a bucket and trying to lift himself up by the handle. (Winston Churchill)

TAXES   In levying taxes and in shearing sheep it is well to stop when you get down to the skin. (Austin O'Malley)

TEA   Tea is the magic key to the vault where my brain is kept. (Frances Hardinge)

TEA   Tea time is a chance to slow down, pull back and appreciate our surroundings. (Letitia Baldrige)

TEA   There is something in the nature of tea that leads us into a world of quiet contemplation of life. (Lin Yutang)

TEACHER   Teaching is not a lost art, but the regard for it is a lost tradition. (Jacques Barzun)

TEACHER A teacher can never truly teach unless he is still learning himself. A lamp can never light another lamp unless it continues to burn its own flame. The teacher who has come to the end of his subject, who has no living traffic with his knowledge but merely repeats his lesson to his students, can only load their minds, he cannot quicken them. (R Tagore)

TEACHER A teacher who establishes rapport with the taught, becomes one with them, learns more from them than he teaches them. He who learns nothing from his disciples is, in my opinion, worthless. Whenever I talk with someone I learn from him. I take from him more than I give him. (M Gandhi)

TEACHER I never teach my pupils, I only attempt to provide the conditions in which they can learn. (Albert Einstein)

TEACHER It is the supreme art of the teacher to awaken joy in creative expression and knowledge. (Albert Einstein)

TEACHER The role of the teacher is like the proverbial 'ladder', it is used by everyone to climb up in life, but the ladder itself stays in its place. (APJ Abdul Kalam)

TEACHER ☺ A teacher's day is half bureaucracy, half crisis, half monotony and one-eighth epiphany. Never mind the arithmetic. (Susan Ohanion)

TEACHER ☺ No wonder the teacher knows so much, she has the book. (EW Howe)

TEACHING A professor is one who talks in someone else's sleep. (WH Auden)

TEACHING I have not taught people in 50 years what my father taught by example in one week. (Mario Cuomo)

TEAM No bird soars too high, if he soars with his own wings. (William Blake)

TEAM   No one can whistle a symphony. It takes an orchestra to play it. (HE Luccock)

TEAM   Two heads are better than one, not because either is infallible, but because they are unlikely to go wrong in the same direction. (CS Lewis)

TEASING When the mouse laughs at the cat there is a hole nearby. (Nigerian proverb)

TECHNOLOGY   The difference between technology and slavery is that slaves are fully aware that they are not free. (NN Taleb)

TECHNOLOGY   If it keeps up, man will atrophy all his limbs but the push-button finger. (FL Wright)

TECHNOLOGY   Technology is the knack for so arranging the world that we do not experience it. (Max Frisch)

TELEPHONE   The telephone is a good way to talk to people without having to offer them a drink. (Fran Lebowitz)

TELEPHONE   The telephone is the greatest nuisance among conveniences, the greatest convenience among nuisances. (RS Lynd)

TELEVISION   TV makes it so easy to postpone living for another half hour.(Bill McKibben)

TEMPTATION   The only way to get rid of temptation is to yield to it. Resist it, and your soul grows sick with longing for the things it has forbidden to itself. (Oscar Wilde)

THEOLOGY   Theology being the work of males, original sin was traced to the female. (Barbara Tuchman)

THINK   There is no expedient to which a man will not resort to avoid the real labor of thinking. (Robert B. Cialdini)

THOUGHT Do not allow negative thoughts to enter your mind for they are the weeds that strangle confidence. (Bruce Lee)

THOUGHT Just as there is no loss of basic energy in the universe, so no thought or action is without its effects, present or ultimate, seen or unseen, felt or unfelt. (Norman Cousins)

THOUGHT Just because you are doing something wrong, doing it more intensely is not going to help. (Vince Lombardi)

THOUGHT The ancestor to every action is a thought. (Emerson)

THOUGHT The glow of one warm thought is to me worth more than money. (Thomas Jefferson)

THOUGHT The greatest weapon against stress is our ability to choose one thought over another. (William James)

THOUGHT The highest possible stage in moral culture is when we recognise that we ought to control our thoughts. (Charles Darwin)

THOUGHT There is nothing either good or bad, but thinking makes it so. (Hamlet)

THOUGHTS   All truly great thoughts are conceived while walking. (Friedrich Nietzsche)

THOUGHTS   Change your thoughts and you change your world. (Norman Vincent Peale)

THOUGHTS   Few people think more than two or three times a year, I have made an international reputation for myself by thinking once or twice a week. (GB Shaw)

THOUGHTS   If we were all to be judged by our thoughts, the hills would be swarming with outlaws. (J Sigurjonsson)

THOUGHTS   It is alright to have a train of thoughts, if you have a terminal. (Bowker)

THRONE   A throne is only a bench covered with velvet. (Napolean Bonaparte)

TIME   If time travel is possible, where are the tourists from the future. (Stephen Hawking)

TIME   Morning are far wiser than evening. (Russian Proverb)

TIME   There are decades where nothing happens; and there are weeks where decades happen. (Vladimir Lenin)

TIME   Are you "spending" your time or "investing" your time? (Carrie Wilkerson)

TIME   One can never change the past, only the hold it has on you. (Merle Shain)

TIME   They deem me mad because I will not sell my days for gold, and I deem them mad because they think my days have a price. (K. Gibran)

TIME   Time is a created thing. To say 'I don't have time', is like saying, 'I don't want to'. (Lao Tzu)

TIME   To use the past to justify the present is bad enough- but it is just as bad to use the present to justify the past. (Amitav Ghosh)

TIME   You never know beforehand what people are capable of, you have to wait, give it time, it's time that rules, time is our gambling partner on the other side of the table and it holds all the cards of the deck in its hand, we have to guess the winning cards of life, our lives. (José Saramago)

TIME ☺   Morning is wonderful. Its only drawback is that it comes at such an inconvenient time of day. (Glen Cook)

TIME   A man who dares to waste one hour of time has not discovered the value of life. (Charles Darwin)

TIME   And in today already walks tomorrow. (ST Coleridge)

TIME   Do nothing secretly ; for Time sees and hears all things, and discloses all. (Sophocles)

TIME   Future is what matters, because one never reaches it, but always stays in the present. (Sylvia Plath)

TIME   A man who dares to waste one hour of time has not discovered the value of life. (Charles Darwin)

TIME   I think the older I get , the more I realize that the ultimate luxury is time. (Michael Kors)

TIME   I wasted time, and now does time waste me. (William Shakespeare)

TIME   If we take care of the moments, the years will take care of themselves. (Maria Edgeworth)

TIME   No man is rich enough to buy back his past. (Oscar Wilde)

TIME   That is what happens when you free people from the restraints of time. They make their own rigid schedule. (K Higashino)

TIME   The future is no more uncertain than the present. (Walt Whitman)

TIME   The older one becomes, the quicker the present fades into sepia and the past looms up in glorious technicolour. (Beryl Bainbridge)

TIME   The time is always right to do what is right. (MLK Jr.)

TIME   The trouble with our times is that the future is not what it used to be. (Paul Valery)

TIME   Time goes, you say? Ah, no ! Alas time stays, we go. (HA Dobson)

TIME   Time you enjoy wasting is not wasted time. (MT Curtin)

TIME   We all have our time machines. Some take us back, they are called memories. Some take us forward, they are called dreams. (J Irons)

TIME   We are tomorrow's past. (Mary Webb)

TOIL   I am a great believer in luck, and I find the harder I work, the more I have of it. (Stephen Leacock)

TOLERANCE   The test of courage comes when we are in the minority. The test of tolerance comes when we are in the majority. (RW Sockman)

TRADITION   It takes an endless amount of history to make even a little tradition. (Henry James)

TRADITION   Don't ever take a fence down until you know the reason it was put up. (GK Chesterton)

TRAVEL Traveling- it leaves you speechless, then turns you into a storyteller. (Ibn Battuta)

TRAVEL   I dislike feeling at home when I am abroad. (George Bernard Shaw)

TRAVEL   I have found that there ain't no surer way to find out whether you like people or hate them than to travel with them. (Mark Twain)

TRAVEL   Not all those who wander are lost. (JRR Tolkien)

TRAVEL   The real voyage of discovery consists not in seeking new landscapes, but in having new eyes. (Marcel Proust)

TRAVEL   The traveler sees what he sees, the tourist sees what he has come to see. (GK Chesterton)

TRAVEL   There are no foreign lands. It is the traveler only who is foreign. (RL Stevenson)

TRAVEL   Travelling- it leaves you speechless, then turns you into a storyteller. (Ibn Battuta)

TROUBLE Wise are they who have learned these truths : Trouble is temporary. Time is tonic. Tribulation is a test tube. (WA Ward)

TRUST   Be courteous to all, but intimate with few, and let those few be well tried before you give them your confidence. (George Washington)

TRUST   I don't trust anyone who doesn't laugh. (Maya Angelou)

TRUST   If you can build trust then you can build relations. (Axel Koster)

TRUST   When someone shows you who they are, believe them the first time. (Maya Angelou)

TRUST   If you think you have someone eating out of your hand, it is a good idea to count your fingers. (Martin Buxbaum)

TRUST   Me, I am dishonest, and you can always trust a dishonest man to be dishonest. Honestly, it's the honest ones you have to watch out for. (Johnny Depp)

TRUST   Show me a man who cannot bother to do little things and I will show you a man who cannot be trusted to do big things. (LD Bell)

TRUST   The best way to find out if you can trust somebody is to trust them. (Ernest Hemingway)

TRUST   We are inclined to believe those whom we do not know because they have never deceived us. (Samuel Johnson)

TRUST   Whoever is careless with the truth in small matters, cannot be trusted with important matters. (Albert Einstein)

TRUTH   Sometimes people don't want to hear the truth because they don't want their illusions destroyed. (Friedrich Nietzsche)

TRUTH   The truth will set you free, but first, it will piss you off. (Gloria Steinem)

TRUTH   Truth is ever to be found in simplicity, and not in the multiplicity and confusion of things. (Isaac Newton)

TRUTH   Unthinking respect for authority is the greatest enemy of truth. (Albert Einstein)

TRUTH   When you shoot an arrow of truth, dip its point in honey. (Arab proverb)

TRUTH ☺ It is perfectly monstrous the way people go about nowadays saying things against one, behind one's back, that are absolutely and entirely true. (Oscar Wilde)

TRUTH   Facts are many, but the truth is one. (RN Tagore)

TRUTH   If you tell the truth, you don't have to remember anything. (Mark Twain)

TRUTH   If you want to be thought a liar, always tell the truth. (LP Smith)

TRUTH   In a room where people unanimously maintain a conspiracy f silence, one word of truth sounds like a pistol shot. (C Milosz)

TRUTH   Man is least himself when he talks in his own person. Give him a mask, and he will tell you the truth. (Oscar Wilde)

TRUTH   The truth will set you free, but first it will piss you off. (Gloria Steinem)

TRUTH   The very concept of objective truth is fading out of the world. Lies will pass into history. (George Orwell)

TRUTH   To be persuasive, we must be believable. To be believable, we must be credible. To be credible, we must be truthful. (Edward R. Murrow)

TRUTH   Sometimes people don't want to hear the truth, because they don't want their illusions destroyed. (Nietzsche)

TRUTH   To be outspoken is easy when you do not wait to speak the complete truth.

TV Watching television is like taking black spray paint to your third eye. (Bill Hicks)

TV I find television very educating. Every time somebody turns on the set, I go into the other room and read a book. (Groucho Marx)

TV Men don't care what is on TV. They only care what else is on TV. (Jerry Seinfled)

UNDERSTANDING Understanding seems to be a very complicated notion. (Roger Schank)

UNIVERSE The universe is run exactly on the lines of a cafeteria. Unless you claim—mentally—what you want, you may sit and wait forever. (Emmet Fox)

UNIVERSE I believe a leaf of grass is no less than the journey-work of the stars. (Walt Whitman)

UNIVERSE What do you feel when you look out at those galaxies? If you go out into a desert or up in the mountains where the sky is clear, you see this colossal affair that you are involved in. It makes a lot of people feel very small, but is should not. It should make you feel as big as it is, because it is all inseparably connected with what you call you. (Alan Watts)

VALUE Nothing is more useful than water: but it will purchase scarcely anything; scarcely anything can be had in exchange for it. A diamond, on the contrary, has scarcely any use-value; but a very great quantity of other goods may frequently be had in exchange for it. (Adam Smith)

VALUE The best things in life are free. The second-best are very expensive. (Coco Chanel)

VALUE When you pay high for the priceless, you are getting it cheap. (J Duveen)

VALUE   Nothing can have value without being an object of utility. (Karl Marx)

VC The biggest secret in venture capital is that the best investment in a successful fund equals or outperforms the entire rest of the fund combined. (Peter Thiel)

VERBOSE ☺   Some people approach every problem with an open mouth. (Adlai Stevenson)

VETERINARIAN The best doctor in the world is a veterinarian. He can't ask his patients what is the matter-he's got to just know. (Will Rogers)

VICE ☺   The problem with people who have no vices is that generally, you can be pretty sure they are going to have some pretty annoying virtues. (Elizabeth Taylor)

VICTORY Once you hear the details of victory, it is hard to distinguish it from a defeat. (Jean-Paul Sartre)

VIOLENCE From pacifist to terrorist, each person condemns violence- and then adds one cherished case in which it may be justified. (Gloria Steinem)

VIRTUE   Virtue and Happiness are Mother and Daughter. (B Franklin)

VIRTUE   Man cannot be uplifted ; he must be seduced into virtue. (Don Marquis)

VISION   Our task now is not to fix the blame for the past, but to fix the course for the future. (John F Kennedy)

VISION   Vision is perhaps our greatest strength. It has kept us alive to the power and continuity of thought through the centuries, it makes us peer into the future and lends shape to the unknown. (Li Ka-shing)

VISION   Vision is the art of seeing what is invisible to others. (Jonathan Swift)

WAGE $ You don't get paid for the hour. You get paid for the value you bring to the hour. (Jim Rohn)

WAGE   I don't pay good wages because I have a lot of money ; I have a lot of money because I pay good wages. (Robert Bosch)

WALK   If you are in a bad mood go for a walk. If you are still in a bad mood go for another walk. (Hippocrates)

WALK   Walk as if you are kissing the earth with your feet. (Thich Nhat Hanh)

WALKING All truly great thoughts are conceived while walking. (Friedrich Nietzsche)

WAR   God created war so that Americans would learn geography. (Mark Twain)

WAR   Older men declare war. But it is the youth that must fight and die. (Herbert Hoover)

WATER   Dance with the waves, move with the sea. Let the rhythm of the water set your soul free. (CA Martine)

WATER   When the well is dry, they know the worth of water. (Benjamin Franklin)

WEAKNESS   Sometimes you don't realize your own strength until you come face to face with your greatest weakness. (Susan Gale)

WEALTH   I think everybody should get rich and famous and do everything they ever dreamt of so they can see that it is not the answer. (Jim Carrey)

WEALTH   If wealth was the inevitable result of hard work and enterprise, every woman in Africa would be a millionaire. (George Monbiot)

WEALTH   Wealth is the slave of a wise man. The master of a fool. (Seneca)

WEALTH   You are not wealthy until you have something money can't buy. (Garth Brooks)

WIFE □   A psychiatrist asks a lot of expensive questions your wife asks for nothing. (Joey Adams)

WINNING It is not the will to win that matters- everyone has that. It is the will to prepare to win that matters. (PB Bryant)

WISDOM   It requires wisdom to understand wisdom : The music is nothing if the audience is deaf. (Walter Lippmann)

WISDOM   Knowledge is being aware that fire can burn ; wisdom is remembering the blister. (Leo Tolstoy)

WISDOM   Knowledge is flour, but wisdom is bread. (Austin O'Malley)

WISDOM   Knowledge is proud that he has learned so much. Wisdom is humble that he knows not more. (William Cowper)

WISDOM   Never mistake knowledge for wisdom. One helps you make a living ; the other helps you make a life. (Eleanor Roosevelt)

WISDOM   Science is organized knowledge. Wisdom is organized life. (Immanuel Kant)

WISDOM   The doorstep to the temple of wisdom is a knowledge of our own ignorance. (B Franklin)

WISDOM   The wise man questions the wisdom of others because he questions his own, the foolish man because it is different from his own. (Leo Stein)

WISDOM   A wise man never knows all, only fools know everything. (African proverb)

WISDOM   He dares to be a fool, and that is the first step in the direction of wisdom. (JG Huneker)

WISDOM   Knowledge is learning something every day. Wisdom is letting go of something every day. (Zen proverb)

WISDOM   Knowledge speaks, but wisdom listens. (Jimi Hendrix)

WISDOM   Stoicism is the wisdom of madness and cynicism the madness of wisdom. (Bergen Evans)

WISDOM   The invariable mark of wisdom is to see the miraculous in the common. (RW Emerson)

WISDOM   The only true wisdom is in knowing you know nothing. (Socrates)

WISDOM   Wisdom is not a product of schooling but of the lifelong attempt to acquire it. (Albert Einstein)

WISDOM   Wisdom is seeing something in a non-habitual manner. (William James)

WISDOM   The art of being wise is the art of knowing what to overlook. (William James)

WISH   Men are nearly always willing to believe what they wish. (Julius Caesar)

WIT   Wit is educated insolence. (Aristotle)

WIT   Wit is the sudden marriage of ideas which, before their union, were not perceived to hae any relation. (Mark Twain)

WOMAN   A woman's guess is much more accurate than a man's certainty. (R Kipling)

WOMAN   I just love bossy women. I could be around them all day. To me, bossy is not a pejorative term at all. It means somebody is passionate and engaged and ambitious and does not mind leading. (Amy Poehler)

WOMAN   No woman really wants a man to carry her off; she only wants him to want to do it. (Elizabeth Peters)

WOMAN ☺ A woman without a man is like a fish without a bicycle. (Gloria Steinem)

WOMAN   Behind every great man is a woman rolling her eyes. (Jim Carrey)

WOMAN   No matter how happily a woman may be married, it always pleases her to discover that there is a nice man who wishes she were not. (HL Mencken)

WOMEN   Women must pay for everything. They do get more glory than men for comparable feats. But they also get more notoriety when they crash. (Amelia Earhart)

WOMEN   For most of history, Anonymous was a woman. (Virginia Woolf)

WOMEN   After about 20 years of marriage, I am finally starting to scratch the surface of what women want. And I think the answer lies somewhere between conversation and chocolate. (Mel Gibson)

WOMEN   God made man stronger but not necessarily more intelligent. He gave women intuition and femininity. And, used properly, that combination easily jumbles the brain of any man I have ever met. (Farrah Fawcet)

WOMEN   Nobody will ever win the battle of the sexes. There is too much fraternizing with the enemy. (Henry Kissinger)

WOMEN   On one issue, at least, men and women agree : they both distrust women. (HL Mencken)

WOMEN   Whatever women do, they must do twice as well as men to be thought half as good. Luckily this is not difficult. (C Whitton)

WOMEN   Women are the only exploited group in history to have been idealized into powerlessness. (Erica Jong)

WOMEN   Women in business are a problem, if you treat them like men they start complaining, if you treat them like women, wife may find out. (Evan Esar)

WOMEN   Women who seek to be equal with men lack ambition. (Timothy Leary)

WONDER When you are playful, you are capable of wonder, awe. And those are the really religious qualities- to be able to feel wonder, to be able to feel alive, to be able to be exhilarated with the beauty that surrounds you. So many flowers, so many colours. (Osho)

WORD   Colors fade, temples crumble, empires fall, but wise words endure. (Edward Thorndike)

WORDPLAY ☺   A thesaurus is great. There is no other word for it. (Ross Smith)

WORDPLAY ☺   I believe a person can be full of contradictions. And I also believe that they can't. (J Burton)

WORDPLAY ☺   I regret rubbing ketchup in my eyes, but that is Heinz sight. (Nick Helm)

WORDPLAY ☺   Someone stole my anti-depressants. Whoever they are, I hope they are happy. (Richard Stott)

WORK   There is no greater thing you can do with your life and your work than follow your passions- in a way that serves the world and you. (Richard Branson)

WORK   Anyone can do any amount of work provided it isn't the work he is supposed to be doing at the moment. (Robert Benchley)

WORK   Anyone can do any amount of work, provided it is not the work he is supposed to be doing at the moment. (Robert Benchley)

WORK   Every man's work, whether it be literature or music or pictures or architecture or anything else, is always a portrait of himself. (Samuel Butler)

WORK ☺   I like work, it fascinates me. I can sit and look at it for hours. (Jerome K Jerome)

WORK   If you can keep hope and worry balanced, they will drive a project forward the same way your two legs drive a bicycle forward. (Paul Graham)

WORK   You think you can see light at the end of the tunnel, but it's only some bugger with a torch bringing you more work. (David Brent)

WORK   Better a little which is well done, than a great deal imperfectly. (Plato)

WORK   If you don't want to work, you have to work to earn enough money so that you won't have to work. (Ogden Nash)

WORK   The highest reward that God gives us for good work is the ability to do better work. (Elbert Hubbard)

WORK   We work to eat to get the strength to work to eat to get the strength to work. (John Dos Passos)

WORK   Work expands to fill the time available for its completion. (CN Parkinson)

WORK   Work is love made visible. And if you cannot work with love but only with distaste, it is better that you should leave your work and sit at the gate of the temple and take alms of those who work with joy. (K Gibran)

WORK   Work is the greatest thing in the world, so we should always save some of it for tomorrow. (Don Herold)

WORLD   The dangerous clashes of the future are likely to arise from the interaction of Western arrogance, Islamic intolerance, and Sinic assertiveness. (Samuel P. Huntington)

WORRY   If you want to test your memory, try to recall what you were worrying about one year ago today. (EJ Coffman)

WORRY   We consume our tomorrows fretting about our yesterdays. (Persius)

WORRY   If you want to fly, give up everything that weighs you down. (Buddha)

WORRY   It's not the load that breaks you down, it's the way you carry it. (Lena Horne)

WORSHIP Better than worshipping gods is obedience to the laws of righteousness. (Buddha)

WORTH   After I am dead I would rather have men ask why Cato has no monument than why he had one. (Cato the Elder)

WORTH   No one is useless in this world who lightens the burdens of another. (Charles Dickens)

WRITING Start writing, no matter what. The water does not flow until the faucet is turned on. (Louis L'Amour)

WRITING What I like in a good author isn't what he says, but what he whispers. (LP Smith)

WRITING Writing is a form of therapy ; sometimes I wonder how all those who do not write, compose or paint can manage to escape the madness, melancholia, the panic fear which is inherent in a human situation. (Graham Greene)

WRITING   When you write you lay out a line of words that is a miner's pick, a woodcarver's gouge, a surgeon's probe. You wield it, and it digs a path you follow. Soon you find yourself deep in new territory. (Annie Dillard)

YOUTH   There is nothing so pitiful as a young cynic because he has gone from knowing nothing to believing nothing. (Maya Angelou)

Youth   Age considers, youth ventures. (R Tagore)